The River People

Philip Wayre is one of Britain's outstanding conservationists, a Fellow of the Zoological Society of London, a member of the Survival Service Commission of the International Union for the Conservation of Nature and Natural Resources (IUCN), a member of the Council of the Fauna Preservation Society and of the Advisory Panel of the World Wildlife Fund.

He is particularly noted for his success in breeding stocks of endangered species. He has the only captive breeding groups of Alpine ibex and roe deer in Britain, and has bred the common otter sixteen times – the only captive breeding success in this country in the present century. He is also founder and honorary director of the Otter Trust which he set up at the Norfolk Wildlife Park at Great Witchingham; it now has its own headquarters at Earsham where many of the otters in this book can be seen.

The
River People

Philip Wayre

Fontana/Collins

TO MY WIFE JEANNE

First published by William Collins Sons & Co. Ltd
and the Harvill Press 1976
First issued in Fontana 1977

Copyright © Philip Wayre 1976

Made and printed in Great Britain by
William Collins Sons & Co. Ltd, Glasgow

Contents

ACKNOWLEDGEMENTS

I am glad to take this opportunity of thanking most sincerely Ken and Julie Scriven without whose help and generous hospitality the Malayan venture would not have been possible. I also wish to thank Bill Macveigh, Ken Sims, Aw Joon Wah and Mike Oliver for their invaluable help and encouragement while we were in Malaysia.

Introduction

Characters in order of appearance.

My otter family at the Norfolk Wildlife Park has grown into a large one over the years and because just as in human families it is not always easy to recall which youngster was born of which parents, let alone who was married to whom, I hope the following summary will help the reader to follow the story.

Chapter 1
Limpet, a North American otter *Lutra canadensis* and the first otter I kept.

Chapter 2
Rollo and Winkle, both North American otters, and responsible for the first of our breeding successes.

Chapter 3
Gutsy and Ripple, both one of the several Asiatic races of the European otter, thought to be *Lutra l. barang* from Thailand.
Rhum and Rhona, brother and sister, and the first of Gutsy and Ripple's progeny.

Chapter 4
Ginger, a British otter *Lutra l. lutra,* caught in a coypu trap in Norfolk.
Gobble, her first son.
Fury, a British otter, found forsaken as a cub on the Isle of Mull and hand-reared by Mrs Innocent, who later gave her to me.

Chapter 5
Lucy and Kate, British otter cubs born to Ginger and her son Gobble (see Chapter 4).

Chapter 6
Cockle and Clam, Gutsy and Ripple's second litter.

Chapter 8
Oscar and Mango, tame Indian smooth-coated otters *Lutra (Lutrogale) perspicillata*, and Freckie, a tame Asian short-clawed otter *Amblonyx c. cinerea* purchased as adults from a film company.
Kuala, a male Asian short-clawed otter, obtained from Kuala Lumpur Zoo as a mate for Freckie.
Mouse, Kuala and Freckie's first cub.
Also in this chapter Grishkin, my tame European lynx *Felis lynx*.

Chapter 9
A pair of young Indian smooth-coated otters, Tanjong and Rhu, purchased from a Chinese businessman on the Island of Langkawi, Malaysia.

Chapter 10
Rompin, a little female Asian short-clawed otter cub purchased from a Malay businessman outside the town of Rompin on the east coast of Malaya.
Rolly, a tame young male Asian short-clawed otter obtained by Bill Macveigh as a mate for Rompin, together with three more pairs of the same species, Woolly and Jalan, Ulu and Thamar, Tambun and Kechil.

1. Limpet my Canadian Otter

The first otter I ever kept came from America. I called her Limpet. She was a North American otter who had been kept in captivity by Art Hoffman of Kansas City. At the time of her arrival I was making a film which included an otter sequence and to obtain it had wired in a large area of water with surrounding reed beds, osier thickets and sedges which had taken over some disused gravel workings.

On fine days we used to take Limpet, shut in her sleeping box, down to the set and release her. During filming much time is spent waiting for a particular thing to happen, so I had plenty of opportunity to study Limpet's behaviour in the comparative freedom of the large enclosure.

First, I learned that she did not like to remain in the water for more than half an hour or so at a time before she came ashore to dry herself by wriggling and writhing on the rough grass at the water's edge. There she would lie flat on her belly, sweeping her head from side to side to dry her neck and chin before squirming to and fro on her back, her four feet in the air. From this position she sometimes sat up to groom the soft fur of her underbelly, her body forming a loop and demonstrating the remarkable flexibility of an otter's spine.

Next, I learned about her different methods of diving and the reasons for them. Her normal dive was quite shallow. Swimming along with just her head showing, she slipped quietly beneath the surface leaving scarcely a ripple, only a chain of bubbles rising to show her direction.

There were eels in the pool and, as with all otters, hunting them was a favourite pastime. To get to the bottom in twenty feet of water she had to dive deep, rolling over porpoise-like in a graceful curve, her rudder following her body to complete the arc. A column of bubbles rose from the depths where I could visualize her rooting in the mud, her sensitive whiskers responding to every movement of her slippery quarry as she searched the murky water at the bottom of the pond.

In midsummer the rising temperature produced a sudden explosion of green algae. Almost overnight the clear water became as green as pea soup, but even under those conditions Limpet still caught eels. Sometimes I threw a live one to her and watched her dive in pursuit. It seemed impossible that she could ever find such an elusive quarry with only a few inches of visibility but find it she always did, even though she sometimes had to dive several times before being successful.

If her suspicions were aroused, Limpet adopted the 'I'm watching you' position, remaining motionless and upright in the water with her head and neck well clear of the surface to get a better view. From this position she could sink silently straight down, leaving scarcely a ring to show where she had been. If badly frightened, she crash-dived with a mighty splash.

During the summer when the vegetation round the disused gravel pits grew tall and rank, when swallows and sand-martins skimmed the water and reed warblers rasped their monotonous song in the dense thickets of phragmites, life around and in the water bustled with feverish activity as every living thing strove to complete its breeding cycle before the onset of autumn.

Always inquisitive, Limpet made the most of her frequent visits to the pits. A pair of Canada geese, wanderers from one of the big estates in Norfolk, had made their nest on a small island where in due time four goslings hatched.

At first the goose brooded them beneath the soft feathers of her breast and flanks, the gander standing guard nearby. But as they became hungry and more active the family set sail, the goose in the van followed by the flotilla of grey goslings bobbing along like corks with the gander bringing up the rear. The sonorous cronks of the adults echoed like the sirens of tugs on the Thames as they manoeuvred their charges.

This was too much for Limpet who, having viewed the convoy, slipped quietly under to launch a torpedo attack from the depths. Watching from the bank I saw her surface close to one of the goslings but before she could do anything the gander surged through the water towards her with wings flailing, hissing with rage, his long neck snaking forward. Limpet was terrified and dived with all the speed she could muster. The Canada goose family sailed on, cronking their victory to the flock grazing on the water meadows beyond the Wensum River.

Sometimes Limpet vanished, remaining hidden for an hour or more, and I began to understand how easily an otter can hide and remain invisible when it may be only a few yards away. Clumps of sedge grew at the margin of the pool, their tall leaves of single spikes hanging over to form arches beneath which the water lapped in heavy shadows. Lying submerged in some dark recess with only the top of her flat head above the surface, her nostrils just clear of the water, Limpet could see without being seen and silently sink to slip away unnoticed.

Able to burrow when necessary, North American otters do not appear to be great diggers, though Limpet always enlarged any rat hole she came across, pushing her muzzle into the soil and scrabbling with her front paws, and no doubt in the wild she would dig out a breeding holt when the time came.

At the moment, however, she found the tangle of summer growth more exciting. Lying flat and pushing with her hind feet, she ploughed her way beneath the mat of dead grass, docks, thistles and brambles, the moving hump of vegetation showing her whereabouts. Down there in the damp darkness she sometimes found a brood of young field voles hidden in their nest of dried grass stems. She ate them with relish, pushing her head up into the daylight, champing noisily. Theirs was a quick end; to frogs, which she also found from time to time, she was less kind. Bringing the poor thing out into the open she dropped it, then prodded it with her muzzle to make it jump, running in pursuit to repeat the game. Often she behaved like a terrier with a rat, throwing it into the air time and again before settling down to eat it. Then she held the frog between her front paws and chewed it in the side of her mouth rather like a dog with a bone.

With the coming of winter the scene round the gravel pits changed. The green growth of summer turned russet, the sere stems, flaxen in death, rustled in the cold wind of December. In place of the swallows, fieldfares from the frozen north cried their harsh 'chuck chuck' as they flew overhead and the full-grown Canada goslings and their parents had rejoined the main flock far out on the flooded meadows. Rafts of wild duck spent the day asleep in the centre of the main lake, and the coots had arrived in numbers. The green algae had disappeared and the water-weeds withered so that I could watch Limpet as she swam beneath the surface.

The small pool was the first to freeze in January for it was protected by high banks of soil from the old gravel workings and frost lay in the pocket. At night the stars were bright in the clear sky and flocks of wigeon whistled as they flew in from the coast to feed on the sweet grass of the meadows.

Then the snow came, blanketing the countryside, and after it the frost hardened its grip and ice covered the large lake. Loath to leave their familiar haunt, mallard and coot sat dejectedly waiting for the thaw.

Up to then I had never dared to let Limpet go completely free, for I always felt she was only half tame, that she accepted me as a working partner, but if given the chance would quickly return to the wild state from which she had originally been taken as a young otter in Canada. While never able to pick her up, I usually had no trouble catching her at the end of a day's filming in the big enclosure, for we always transported her in her wooden sleeping box so that she was never handled or frightened. She liked her box and often returned to it, so that when the time came to go home all I had to do was to put an eel or two inside and close the door when she went in. This nearly always worked.

With the countryside in the grip of ice and snow I felt the time had come to allow Limpet to spend a day in freedom. So long as we kept her away from the unfrozen river, we should be able to follow her anywhere. There was little cover left in which she could hide and her dark colour would show up against the white background.

We carried her sleeping box into the filming enclosure and leaving the gate in the fence wide open, let her out. I felt there was just a chance that later on in the day, when she began to feel hungry, she might return so that we could recapture her in the usual way. The alternative would be to catch her in a net which is something all otters hate, and I dislike doing it as it destroys their confidence in us.

After a brief inspection of her familiar surroundings, Limpet found the open gate. Three times she stopped, peering out at the wide countryside 'huffing' with suspicion, and each time she drew back. Finally she passed through it and out into the dazzling white of a snow-covered field. Almost at once she discovered a new game. Pushing her head beneath the snow so that her body became wedge-shaped, she rushed along like an invisible snow plough, sending a white plume into the air which fell over her back.

Sometimes she surfaced, galloped a few paces and then slid along on her tummy. Clearly she liked the snow and found it fun. At the top of the steep bank beside the main pit she paused, then, lying flat, pushed off with her hind feet and went tobogganing down on to the ice below. Picking herself up she set off across the frozen lake running and sliding alternately.

Out in the centre, the mallard rose quacking in alarm, but the coots seemed loath to fly. Instead they began to walk away from her and as she drew nearer they increased speed, only to slip and slide about on the ice like novice skaters. That was too much for Limpet who rushed after them, skidding and slipping herself so that the whole scene quickly developed into a farce, and only at the last minute did the coots reluctantly take wing.

After exploring the main lake, Limpet made her way towards a thick thorn hedge where the snow lay thin on the leeward side. She moved easily beneath the dead bracken and bramble thickets, following the line of the hedge and breaking into a canter whenever a pheasant jumped up, but they were always a few paces ahead of her as they flew to safety.

Coming to another big pit she walked right round it, keeping to the bank, and only ventured on to the ice to cross a narrow inlet. After several hours of freedom she had worked her way back towards the film set and, to my relief, walked in at the open gate without hesitation. There was no need for the net. Tired and hungry, she was only too pleased to go back into her sleeping box.

I described in a previous book *Wind in the Reeds* how I lost Limpet when she chewed her way out of the pen I had built for her. In those days I had little idea how strong otters were and how easily they could tear holes in heavy gauge wire netting. Her escape was responsible for the only time I have ever been otter hunting, for the local hounds met nearby a few days later and I was afraid they might find her and kill her.

At the meet I told the Master about Limpet and he suggested that I spent the day with them, assuring me that if I thought they had found her he would call off the hounds immediately.

They did not find her, but they did find another otter and I wrote thus of the hunt that followed:

'The river here meanders through low-lying water meadows intersected by narrow ditches. Successive dredging operations have left the silt piled on either bank, resulting in a luxuriant growth of thistles, nettles and willow herb. There is no tow-path and fallen willows and rough spinneys of alder and thorn clutter the bank. Hounds worked slowly upstream, leaving the gravel pits which Limpet knew so well on their right; sometimes they followed one of the ditches leading away from the river but without success. As the afternoon wore on, it began to look as though no otters were to be found on this stretch of the river. Two or three hounds were splashing about in a small ditch which divided two meadows, when suddenly an otter dashed out of a clump of thistles and dived into the river.

'I happened to be standing less than ten paces away and

knew at once that it was not Limpet: this otter was too small and pale. Hounds rushed into the water in full cry, swimming back down the river; the followers ran along either bank leaving one or two elderly members of the field leaning on their staffs and gazing down into the water. There they remained quite still, watching, reminding me of herons waiting for a fish. The pack left the river and hunted through a rough alder spinney, then they seemed baffled and fanned out in the meadow beyond. The huntsman called them and led them back to the river, casting on downstream. Suddenly one of the silent watchers upstream caught sight of the otter as it dived under the opposite bank, leaving a tell-tale line of bubbles. He halloa'd and the huntsman ran back with his hounds. So the hunt went on; twice the otter took to the land, but it was always forced to return to the river after a few hundred yards. Several times hounds were at fault and it looked as though their quarry would slip away, but somebody always spotted either the otter's head as it came up for air or the trail of bubbles as it dived.

'After more than an hour it became obvious that it was beginning to tire. Its dives were of shorter duration, it was forced to surface for air more frequently, and it was only swimming from one bank to another downstream in an attempt to find safety. Once it took refuge under the roots of a fallen tree but was dislodged by several men poking about and rattling their sticks under the straggling limbs. Finally in desperation, half-drowned and exhausted, the poor creature dragged its sodden body ashore. Twenty yards out in the meadow it met its end – a young bitch otter weighing fourteen pounds.

'To me it was all rather pointless; the otter was so much more beautiful and interesting alive. While I agree that traps are even more cruel than hunting, I can see no excuse for wanting to kill otters at all. They are enchanting creatures who by their specialized requirements of food, habitat and living space are never likely to become numerous. Furthermore, any damage they do to fishing interests has always been exaggerated and in any event would never be a thousandth part of the destruction caused by pollution, detergents and chemical insecticides. Add the fact that nobody has yet proved that otters do more harm than good, bearing in mind the large number of eels and small rodents they kill, the more logical course would be to give them total protection.

'From that day to this I have had no clue as to Limpet's whereabouts. If she had been caught or killed locally, I think I should have heard as so many neighbours and friends knew her. Sometimes when I lay in bed on a summer's night with the moon up and my windows open, I fancied I heard her far-off whistle down by the river, and in my mind I saw her flat head rise from the depths of the gravel pit and swim away, the ripples shimmering in the moonlight to mark her going.'

Of one thing I was certain, Limpet had fired within me a lasting enthusiasm for otters and next time I determined to keep not one, but a pair, for my most cherished ambition was to breed them in captivity.

The Home Office Committee on Cruelty to Wild Animals, appointed in June 1949, reported in April 1951. Paragraph 316 of its Report started with these words – 'Hunting does undoubtedly involve suffering for the otter, and the degree of it is rather greater than in most other field sports.'

The Committee is to be congratulated on the understatement of the century. Readers will be able to judge for themselves from the factual account of a day's otter hunting related above, but it is difficult to understand what pleasure educated and civilized people can derive from the pursuit of an otter until it is close to drowning and its eventual death in the jaws of the pack.

But there are even more cogent reasons for banning such a cruel sport. The British otter breeds all the year round and newly-born cubs have been found in every month. Therefore it follows that otters are hunted when the females may be heavily pregnant or nursing young and helpless cubs. I can think of no other sport where the quarry is killed, regardless of sex, during the breeding season.

Of course, devotees of otter hunting have glib and quite unproven answers to this charge. They claim they are able to recognize a pregnant bitch and automatically whip off the hounds. I have now bred the common otter nine times in captivity and as will be described have always experienced considerable difficulty in determining whether or not a bitch is pregnant, even when examining her daily at a distance of a few feet. Sometimes it is easier to tell as parturition approaches, for when an otter walks on land the outline of its stomach in profile is concave or arched, except in advanced pregnancy when there is usually a shallow bulge. If a bitch is going to produce more than two cubs the swelling is correspondingly larger.

To observe such a fine detail in the field, especially in an otter swimming and diving in front of a pack of hounds, would be impossible. Otter hunters assert that a pregnant or nursing bitch carries little or no scent, but I know of no scientific evidence to support this contention and indeed they sometimes get killed as do the cubs.

The season for hunting otters in Britain is from April to October, but this has nothing to do with the otter's breeding habits. It is simply that the followers prefer to operate in comfort during the summer months. All the available evidence points to a drastic decline in otters in recent years over almost the whole of Britain, except perhaps in parts of the extreme north-west and Scotland.

Their decline cannot be blamed on hunting nor solely on trapping and shooting, though doubtless all three factors have contributed to it. It seems more likely that the draining of marshes, dredging of rivers and cleaning of their banks, coupled with the enormous increase in every form of human activity connected with waterways, including angling, sailing and rambling, have all taken their toll of the otter's world. Pollution both direct and indirect through the otter's food species as the result of pesticides and industrial waste may well have tipped the balance against its survival. Under these conditions it is ridiculous to suggest that any form of control of the otter population is necessary, for not only is the otter one of our most fascinating and intriguing native mammals, but it is also amongst the rarest and one which, by and large, does little or no damage to man or his interests. The time has come to give legal protection to the otter in this country as has been done for seals, deer, badgers and the majority of birds.

2. First Otter Babies

Otters have been bred only rarely in captivity; indeed up to 1965 there were no known records in Britain during the present century. However the North American otter, the species Limpet belonged to, had been bred regularly on the other side of the Atlantic by at least two naturalists, Art Hoffman and Emil Liers.

Unlike our otter, the North American has a gestation period varying from nine to twelve months; this is due to the phenomenon of delayed implantation of the foetus. After mating, the fertilized egg remains in the female's uterus in the form of a blastocyst and does not begin to develop for some months. Then, triggered by the production of certain hormones, probably connected with the amount of daylight at that particular time of the year, the blastocyst anchors itself to the wall of the womb and from then on development of the foetus continues normally. This arrangement ensures that in this species, though not in others, the cubs are always born at roughly the same season, that is, early in the year.

Presumably this adaptation has survival value in a species which, in the northernmost part of its range, has to cope with very severe winters, for it means that the cubs are well-grown and experienced hunters, able to look after themselves, by the time the snow and ice return the following winter.

After Limpet's escape I determined to obtain a pair of North American otters and to make every effort to breed them. Art Hoffman came to my rescue and soon a very fine dog otter arrived, accompanied by a sprightly young bitch. I had already built two breeding pens to Art's design, but decided they were on the small side for permanent quarters though ideal as maternity pens. So Rollo, as I christened the dog otter, and his wife Winkle occupied the new otter enclosure in the Wildlife

Park. Being quite tame, they were soon a centre of attraction for our visitors.

The following spring I watched them carefully, hoping to notice some sign that they too were aware of the season and that the rising sap was not confined to the willow trees leaning over their pool.

Liers had spoken of the male's complete change in disposition during the mating season and mentioned some males who 'go berserk when they sense interference' and who 'will charge anyone near, whether that individual be man or beast'. He also stated that the male's testicles begin descending in November. I watched in vain; Rollo's testicles showed no sign of change and his temperament remained placid and gentle. Nor did Winkle evince any encouraging symptoms that I could see. They remained the well-behaved, devoted couple. Remembering Liers's statement that he had had 'forty-six males that were never able to breed a female', I was convinced that Rollo was the forty-seventh.

Summer died slowly, to be replaced by the increasing cold and grey drabness of winter. The otters looked sleek and plump in their thick coats. Then came the ice, six inches deep on their pool, but it made no difference to them, they merely kept open a hole a couple of feet in diameter and through it plunged into the freezing water below. At first I was afraid they would run out of breath and drown before they could rediscover the opening, but it never happened, and after a few consecutive frosts I noticed that the water level had dropped away from the ice, leaving a gap of several inches so that the otters could breathe wherever they surfaced.

The ice had hardly disappeared when I fancied I could discern a change in Winkle. Was she a trifle fatter and had her belly a rounded look that wasn't there before and were her movements perceptibly slower?

One January day Roy, our Manager, and I decided to take a closer look. We went to the otters' enclosure and called Winkle out, one of us feeding her while the other observed her profile. After some discussion we decided that to be on the safe side we would move her to one of the maternity pens. Rollo remained alone in the Park, and I fully expected him to pine for his missing mate, but if he felt lonely it didn't affect his appetite.

During February Winkle grew more portly, her belly more pronounced, until in March it rubbed the ground when she walked. The small wooden hut forming her breeding den was filled with fresh dry straw; excitement was mounting. Would we be able to claim the first successful breeding in captivity of any species of otter in Britain this century? As Winkle's appetite increased, we stepped up her rations and gave her the choicest food.

On 27 March she remained all day in her hut and her dinner was untouched. I listened in vain at the door to her den, but no sound came from within, no feeble squeaking of newborn cubs.

The next day the silence continued. I began to get frantic. Had she died? Was that why her food was uneaten? I knew the first rule with any carnivore is never to disturb it with new-born young, for fear the mother will eat her own children. Nobody really knows why this happens, though it's commonly believed that it's her way of protecting them – a kind of unconscious attempt to return them to the safety of her womb. I could bear the suspense no longer; after all, Winkle knew me and just a tiny glimpse was all I needed. Breaking all the rules I crooned her name and slowly and carefully slid back the roof of her den. No sound, no movement from inside; the gap widened to let in the light and there, lying crescent-shaped, was Winkle with three beautiful cubs nuzzling against her warm belly. They lay very still and made no noise; their dark grey coats were dry and velvety. Looking up at me, she made no other move as I slowly slid back the lid. We, or rather Winkle and Rollo, had done it.

For the next two weeks I made sure Winkle was not disturbed, but after that I made regular daily visits to her den and began to handle the cubs. Whenever I attempted to do this she became extremely angry and possessive, so it was necessary to shut her out. Even then I had to keep an eye on her since she was quite likely to slip round behind the den and nip me in the leg. Her sharp teeth penetrated my rubber boots on more than one occasion.

The cubs' eyes began to open at twenty-two days when two narrow slits could just be seen, though it was not until they were thirty-three days old that their eyes were fully open. Sometimes it was not easy to separate Winkle from her cubs and if I wasn't quick enough she would rush into the den, seize a cub by the scruff of the neck and drag it away.

When handled, the cubs whimpered like very young puppies and frequently passed a pungent, evil-smelling milky-coloured fluid from their anal scent glands. The stench was most unpleasant and seemed more persistent than the normal secretion of the adults.

Young otters develop very slowly and the three cubs, which turned out to be two males and a female, were a month old before they were able to lift their heads, and at this age they were still barely able to crawl.

It appears that the North American otter comes into season three to four weeks after giving birth and if unmated will not come into oestrus again until the following spring. Art Hoffman had advised me to keep the male in an adjoining enclosure and to drive the female through to him every day once the cubs were three weeks old until a successful mating had been accomplished. For some reason we were late moving Rollo to the next pen, and it wasn't until thirty days after the birth that Winkle was shut out of her den and driven through the dividing door to be reunited with her husband. Seeing Rollo, she dashed towards him in what we imagined was to be a joyous greeting: instead she flew at him snarling like an enraged tigress and attacked him viciously, getting on top of him and biting his ears and neck. Poor Rollo screamed and trembled, making hardly any attempt to defend himself. We separated them and drove Winkle back into her own enclosure.

Every day we went through the same procedure although by then we knew what to expect and so did Rollo. After a week he would retire to the corner of his pen furthest away from the dividing door the moment he saw us open it and, cowering, would await Winkle's inevitable onslaught. Gradually her attacks became less violent, but still there was not the slightest sign of a return to nuptial bliss. After three weeks we came to the conclusion that Winkle must have come into season before her first reintroduction to Rollo, though I now think this rather unlikely since, if mating does not occur, oestrus is said by Liers to last up to forty days or more.

The theory behind the mating procedure seems sound enough for it is believed that, in the wild, the female leaves her cubs in the safety of the holt or den and swims off in search of her spouse when she feels the urge. After they have mated she returns to her cubs and he continues his bachelor existence. Thus the male does not have to approach the nursery, where his presence would be most unwelcome. That is the theory, but so little is known of the breeding habits of the North American otter in the wild that it may be inaccurate.

By the time the cubs were seven weeks old they were venturing outside their hut, though never straying far from it. Winkle had made a shallow depression in the sand in the shade of a willow bush and there she spent much of the time sleeping, idling in the sun or suckling her young.

I spent many hours watching the family, for I knew that my observations could well be unique, especially when portrayed on film. The cubs suckled frequently, whimpering and squeaking loudly when competing for their mother's favours. They suckled whether Winkle was lying on her side or on her back, as she often preferred, and when their demands irritated her she pushed them away with her front paws. After a bout of suckling she ate the cubs' faeces, stimulating them by licking their hind quarters. I watched her teaching them the drying movements which would soon become so important, encouraging them to rub their bodies from side to side along the sand in snake-like movements.

As the cubs became more adventurous, they often approached the edge of their concrete pool and lay with their heads hanging over the side, sometimes ducking beneath the water. If Winkle happened to notice, she called them away with a low whimpering note, and if they failed to return to her, she ran to them and pushed them back with her front paws, or dragged them to the willow bush by the scruff of the neck as a cat carries its kittens.

Eventually the inevitable happened – the boldest cub leant just a little too far over the side of the pool and lost his balance. In he slipped. He remained afloat looking rather surprised, then began to paddle awkwardly with all four feet. Winkle saw what had happened and quickly dived into the water. She surfaced beside the cub and pushed him along with her muzzle, finally lifting him out by the scruff of the neck.

There is a popular belief, propagated by writer after writer, that the female otter has to encourage her cubs to enter water and then teach them to swim. I think there are various reasons for the origin of this fallacy and the most probable is that if a bitch otter is disturbed with very young cubs, she will endeavour to remove them to safety as quickly as possible and to do this will grab a cub by the scruff and swim away with it.

We must remember that hitherto very few observations had been made on the breeding behaviour of any species of otter and that once a belief of this kind becomes established people tend to look for proof of it.

Winkle certainly did not have to encourage her young to swim; on the contrary she spent quite a lot of time pushing or carrying them away from the water. Nor did they show any fear of the water, still less of putting their heads under it.

Two days after the first cub had taken his involuntary dip, I set up the camera and spent nearly ten hours watching and waiting. One thing soon became clear: the cubs were only permitted to swim when Winkle allowed them to do so and when this happened she encouraged them by leading them to the edge of the pool, diving and surfacing repeatedly in front of them until, one after the other, all three cubs were afloat. They bobbed about like corks, paddling awkwardly, with their tails, unused, held straight out behind them.

If a cub appeared to be having difficulty climbing up the concrete lip of the pool, Winkle would swim up and either push it out or lift it by the scruff. Quite often one of them tried to go for a swim on its own, only to be seized and dragged back to the willow bush.

When the cubs were eight weeks old they were able to run with the same action as an adult otter, the back arched and stomach well clear of the ground. It was at this stage that I watched them eating some of Winkle's meat and meal mixture though they were still suckling regularly. Soon all three were swimming confidently and diving like adults, spending more and more time playing with each other in the water.

I still handled the youngsters daily and they showed no sign of aggressive behaviour until they were nine weeks old when one of them attempted to bite me; thereafter all three gradually became more aggressive when I tried to pick them up.

The cubs were ten weeks old when they started to eat appreciable amounts of solid food; by this time they were getting more independent and Winkle worried less about them. They spent the summer days outside in their enclosure, gambolling and swimming until, exhausted, they returned to sleep in the shade of the willow bush. By the middle of July they began to lose interest in Winkle as a source of food and by the end of the month they were finally weaned.

Much has been written about female otters having to teach their young to catch living food and the cubs' first efforts were something I particularly wanted to witness. They were three and a half months old when I thought Winkle was beginning to lose condition and decided to feed her up. That evening I threw two live eels to her as she lay with her cubs beneath the willow bush. She ate both.

The next evening I threw two more live eels into the pool and Winkle immediately caught one and went ashore to eat it. One of the cubs ran to the pool, slipped into the water and began to pursue the remaining eel. The chase lasted quite a long time, perhaps five minutes before the youngster finally caught it. He took it ashore and started to eat it, beginning at the head in the normal manner. He was obviously enjoying his first quarry when Winkle got up, and calmly took it away and ate it herself. The next evening the same cub pursued and caught another eel far more quickly.

I noted with interest that although the cub had seen an eel only once and then on dry land, it recognized the one in the pool as potential food and immediately chased and caught it without assistance or tuition from its mother. The pursuit and capture of moving prey appears to be innate behaviour in otters.

3. Otters in my House

The small pet shop in London's Edgware Road was squalid even by pet shop standards. Once inside the glass-panelled door one became aware of noise and smell. Cockatoos shrieked, canaries sang, countless small finches twittered to and fro in tiers of overcrowded cages, while on the floor puppies in pens howled and whined away the days of waiting for a new, and one hoped a more sympathetic, owner. Over all hung the pungent odour of urine-soaked sawdust, damp straw and stale food.

From my point of view there was something special about this pet shop because the owner had advertised a pair of young common otters in the classified section of a weekly newspaper. Common otters are found wild in Britain and Europe and in slightly different forms right across Asia to Taiwan in the Far East, but they have never been easy to acquire and for years I had cherished an ambition to breed this fascinating animal in captivity – something which had not been done in this country during the present century. Indeed the last authentic breeding was achieved by A. H. Cocks as long ago as 1881, although I had already successfully bred the North American otters, Rollo and Winkle.

In answer to my enquiry the proprietor of the shop replied that he still had the two otters 'out in the back'. I followed him into an even dingier room behind the shop. A few cages stacked against one wall contained a variety of pathetic creatures whose condition precluded their being seen by prospective customers, but the room was dominated by a desk littered with grubby invoices and a couple of tin lids full of cigarette ends, while against the far wall stood a large and rusting refrigerator. Bending down, the man opened the door of a box-like cage and hustled out a young otter which promptly ran swiftly behind the refrigerator. This was the male, he explained, and quite tame, in fact he often let it have the run of the room. I hoped there was a guard on the back of the fridge for I could visualize what might happen to the otter if the motor suddenly started up when it was hiding inside. Fortunately a herring dangled in a strategic position had the desired result and the little animal shot out and seized it before retiring with it beneath the desk. While it was eating I had a chance to take a good look. The otter was about twenty inches long including his nine-inch tail, and I reckoned he probably weighed about five pounds, so he was well under half-grown and unlikely to be more than four or five months old. He champed the fish noisily, holding it down with the claws of his webbed front feet and I could see the pale whitish fur beneath his neck and the five clumps of long stiff white whiskers, two sprouting each side of his nose, with two more further back beneath his neck and a fifth below the middle of his chin. His head was broad and rather flat, his ears tiny, and his naked nose small with that characteristic wavy line shaped rather like a shallow W where it joined the fur – the rhinarium as it is called. This detail proved that although the animal had been imported from Bangkok, it was beyond doubt a common otter of an Asiatic race.

'Can you pick him up?' I asked the shopkeeper. 'You can try but he's inclined to nip.' I decided not to try and between us we managed to coax him into a small wooden box, for I had already decided this was an opportunity not to be missed despite the rather high price.

'What about the female?' I asked. 'She's smaller and not so tame,' he replied, opening another cage. I looked inside and sure enough a smaller and slimmer otter lay curled up in the straw. She 'huffed' a warning snort as I put out my hand to close the lid. I felt she was probably about the same age as the male and might even be his sister, since it is not unusual for more than one cub to be caught at the same time. A few minutes later I was heading out of London with the two otters in their boxes safely on the rear seat of the car.

Back in Norfolk I should have to think seriously about how I was to keep them, for plainly they were too young and too recently imported from a hot climate to be put straight out in one of our open breeding enclosures in the middle of February. On the other hand I had misgivings about keeping otters in the house. True, otters are above all contact animals that need constant companionship and attention but they are also aquatic and born travellers, so the confines of a house can never fulfil their needs. In the end I decided on a compromise, keeping them in a heated shed complete with a shallow tank of water during the day, but bringing them into the house in the evenings.

The male soon took over our living-room, exploring behind the sofa, prying in the log basket and generally enjoying his strange new world. His appetite was prodigious, though he preferred fresh fish or pieces of raw chicken or rabbit to the special mix which has always formed the basis of my otters' diet. It consists of raw minced beef, biscuit meal, a little bran and rolled oats, some bone meal, yeast, a raw egg, cod-liver oil, milk and grated carrot. Eels are a luxury and the favourite food of every otter I have known, while dead day-old chicks are usually popular as well as nutritious.

Gutsy, as he became known, soon ate almost anything we offered, but the little female whom we called Ripple was far more fastidious. Also she was more nervous and it was several weeks before she dared leave the security of the travelling box I used for carrying them to and fro. Even the sight and smell of a fresh herring lying a foot or two away from the open door would rarely tempt her out. But we persevered, and in the end she would wait until she thought nobody was looking and then slip silently across the carpet to her favourite hideout under the desk. Her svelte brown body was much leaner than Gutsy's and she moved with sinuous snake-like stealth, never leaving the cover of some piece of furniture to venture across the open floor.

Otters are usually very easy to house-train and Gutsy and Ripple were no exception. All one needs is a cat-tray filled with

sand upon which a small quantity of otter droppings (spraint)
is placed. If the tray is put on a newspaper in a quiet corner of
the room there should be few accidents, but the newspaper is
necessary owing to the manner in which an otter relieves itself.
Like badgers they have traditional lavatories or spraining
spots and in the wild such places are often used by generations of otters over many years. Sometimes a certain rock just
above river level will be a favourite place, while a stone or
ledge beneath a bridge or below a weir is often equally popular.
Otter spraint is somewhat sticky and the lingering odour helps
to provide continuity, since an otter prefers to go where an
otter has already been. In a room, the sand-tray represents
such a spraining site and an otter wishing to use it will first
smell the sand then turn round and, with tail raised, reverse
into it before relieving itself – sometimes the aim is not all it
might be, hence the need for the newspaper.

Otters are intensely inquisitive animals and their natural
curiosity sometimes leads them into trouble. Gutsy always
investigated everything in the room. First he turned over the
waste-paper basket and rifled through its contents, then
systematically he pulled down anything moveable within his
reach, and since he was a good climber there was little that
wasn't.

Otters are not designed for jumping and most species have
difficulty in getting more than a foot or so into the air if one
counts the height of a jump from the ground to the back feet.
But they make up for it by the extraordinary elasticity of their
body and neck. Gutsy was soon able to haul himself up on top
of the cupboards, chimney-breast and bookshelves. The latter
always intrigued him and he liked to disappear behind the
books, simply pushing two or three out on to the floor when he
wished to reappear and move on.

His climbing ability and insatiable curiosity meant that
things like sewing baskets, vases, bottles, cigarette boxes and
all the usual bric-à-brac of a living-room had to be put out of
his reach. Electric flex was another danger; although he never
made a serious attempt to chew through it, I always felt it

might happen one day, so I pulled all lamp plugs out when he was in the room.

Chairs, too, had to be moved away from tables and desk or he quickly used them as stepping stones to upward exploration. He displayed a remarkable degree of balance, being able to stand up on his hind legs on the arm of a chair using his tail as a counterpoise while he stretched forward trying to reach his next objective.

Like all otters Gutsy was extremely playful and once he became at ease with us he liked constant attention. However, otters also seem to have butterfly brains and nothing held his interest for long, though he did become attached to certain cherished toys. One of these was a small plastic walrus and his favourite pastime was to carry it in his mouth and drop it into a large earthenware pot of water which we kept for him on the stone hearth. He either plunged his head in to retrieve it or twiddled with his front paws and flicked it over the edge, often lying on his back and attempting to juggle with it. Like a kitten he would chase a twist of paper on the end of a length of string, standing on his hind legs and attempting to seize it in his mouth. Pens, pencils, thimbles and corks were all toys of the moment, but no more.

Hide-and-seek behind the cushions on the sofa was another of Gutsy's favourite games, watched from a safe distance and perhaps with envy by timid Ripple. I never managed to pick him up – any attempt always resulted in quite a hard bite. Gutsy's bites eventually became rather a problem, especially with strangers, for he seemed to understand that a well-timed nip would often achieve his objective and if a visitor happened to sit in a chair which he coveted he jumped up and bit without warning! He certainly had no fear of people, rather an aggressiveness which could be quite daunting. Ripple was the opposite, shy and secretive, always on the defensive and sometimes I despaired of ever making any headway with her. Yet imperceptibly she was gaining confidence, though I never guessed that in a few years' time, and despite her diminutive size, both Gutsy and I would have cause to treat her with respect, or for that matter that she would ultimately accept me as a silent onlooker in the most secret moments of an otter's life.

As with so many wild animals otters may be tame and confident with those they know but very nervous or unreliable in the presence of strangers. We soon had a good example of this with Gutsy, for one day a film unit arrived from the BBC to shoot a sequence of him playing in the living-room. They set up their camera and lights while I put all his toys in strategic spots and his bowl of water on the hearth. When all was ready I fetched Gutsy and let him out, not expecting any trouble. He took one look at the film men and shot straight up the chimney, his claws gripping the rough stone-work, for common otters are good climbers. The flue was both large and old so that he had no difficulty in finding a ledge quite high up and almost out of sight and there he lay, refusing to budge. There was no way of reaching him and eventually the men had to retire outside while I waited alone and tried to entice him down.

After twenty minutes of futile effort I joined the men outside and we took it in turns to peer through a window. At last Gutsy decided the coast was clear and reappeared. Creeping quietly into the room I beckoned the men to follow and with considerable care they took up their positions.

Blocking up the chimney was out of the question without making a special frame of wire netting and in any case Gutsy took good care to keep within easy range of his retreat. I threw a small piece of herring into his water pot and he promptly put his head under to retrieve it and began to eat. One by one the lights were switched on and at last the camera began to run. Quick as a flash Gutsy shot up the chimney taking the remains of his fish with him!

The lights were switched off and again we all trooped outside. Half an hour later Gutsy put in a further appearance. Back we crept, slowly the lights came on, but before the camera could be turned on him he disappeared quickly up the chimney. After this third failure the film unit were forced to admit defeat. Wearily they took down their equipment, stowed it in their cars and set off on their journey back to London. Gutsy had won.

The programme director asked if I could shoot the sequence for them and so a few nights later I set up the same scene and fetched Gutsy and Ripple for their usual evening in the house.

As I guessed, Ripple knew at once that things were different; she slipped beneath the desk and lay low. Gutsy seemed more interested in the lighting and camera leads, but at length he ran to his bowl and started to play with his plastic walrus. With some trepidation I switched on the lights and focused the camera, expecting him to dive for cover, but he was too engrossed and continued to play, oblivious of the disturbance, so that I was able to shoot the sequence required.

Unfortunately many people seem to think otters make good pets, but this isn't the case. Certainly they are among the most attractive, engaging and playful animals one could hope to find and one feels instinctively they ought to make good pets. But there are several reasons why they don't. Despite their rubbery and cuddly appearance they do not like being picked up except when very young. They belong to a large group of animals known to zoologists as mustelids which includes stoats, weasels, polecats, badgers, wolverines and others. They all have two things in common, powerful anal scent glands, absent only in the sea otter, and a vicious bite, for their teeth are adapted for crushing bones.

The scent glands are used for marking their territory and it seems likely that an otter can recognize other individuals by their characteristic odour. The glands may also be used in defence since an otter suddenly frightened will emit a powerful smell, and I noticed that Gutsy sometimes did so out of sheer excitement when engaged in a boisterous game. While pungent at the time, the smell is not very persistent though inclined to recur if the room temperature suddenly rises, especially if the pale milky secretion which can be ejected several inches has been sprayed on to chairs or carpet.

The musty smell always reminds me of burnt sugar and it's

not really too unpleasant once one has become used to it. However it is inclined to permeate clothes, and some of our visitors, unaware that we share our home with otters, have wondered why they themselves smelt odd after sitting in our chairs.

An otter's bite can be serious and even in play will sometimes draw blood; moreover many individuals tend to be quick-tempered, while some become unreliable at certain stages of their normal sexual cycle.

Gavin Maxwell's famous Edal, despite her unusual tameness, finally bit her keeper so seriously that he lost two fingers as a result. A friend of mine had an African spotted-necked otter which was exceptionally tame. I remember calling there one morning and while we were sitting talking the otter started to play round my feet. Rolling it over I tickled its tummy and it responded by climbing on to my lap and lay there squirming with pleasure. I thought it quite the most enchanting animal. Two days later and for no apparent reason it bit a girl visitor very badly and shortly after did the same thing to its owner.

Normally gentle, Gutsy and Ripple tended to bite more often and harder as they grew up, especially if thwarted. By now Gutsy turned the scales at just over fourteen pounds to Ripple's eight pounds, for their particular race of common otter, which is found in Eastern Asia, is slightly smaller than its European counterpart. With maturity, though still friendly with us, they lost their desire to be in the house, so I decided the time was ripe to put them out in the Park in an open enclosure.

Their new home had a large pool, plenty of dry land, a roomy cave with a deep layer of dry sand and a dark den which would be closed during the day so they could always be seen, even when sleeping curled up in the cave. There was a hollow tree trunk, rock-work and a chute made from natural sandstone although the slide itself consisted of glazed half-pipes to ensure a smooth and slippery surface. The top of the chute was four feet high and the slide, at a fairly steep angle, ended two feet above the water.

Gutsy took to it at once, running up the rock-work steps to

slither headlong into the pool. Plainly he enjoyed this new game and we knew he used the chute at night as well, for it was always wet in the morning and had tell-tale streaks of sand from his feet.

Our staff soon discovered they could get Gutsy to use the chute whenever they wished by throwing small pieces of herring or whitebait down it, having first enticed him up the steps and on to the top. This was very popular with visitors to the Park, and he became one of the most photographed animals of the entire collection. Gradually, chuting developed into a ritual at half past three every afternoon, at which time an admiring crowd thronged round the enclosure. Gutsy seemed to enjoy his new role and posed at the top of the chute, standing erect on his hind feet while the cameras clicked, then, after a reward of a tidbit, he hurled himself head first down the slide to splash into the pool, repeating the trick half a dozen times or more.

The common otter is by nature a nocturnal prowler and on hot days it was always difficult to wake Gutsy from his afternoon slumbers. After a great deal of coaxing from one of the girls he would get up and yawn, then slowly stroll to the water's edge before slipping in for a swim. Refreshed, he was ready for action, and climbed to the top of the rock-work to take his bow. In time he developed a curious quirk, for he refused to go down the chute for one piece of fish, it had to be two. I felt sure that soon he would demand three pieces, then four and so on, but it never happened; two it was and two it has stayed. Only Gutsy knows why.

Ripple never used the chute in public, though I often caught her at the top during my walks round the Park in the dusk, after everyone had gone home, and I am pretty sure she enjoyed it during the hours of darkness. But during Gutsy's performance she developed her own role. Entering the pool she swam and dived, somersaulted and corkscrewed through the water for her rewards; often swimming beneath the chute when Gutsy was hurtling down. Unable to avoid her, Gutsy would disappear with her in a flurry of foam, and both would surface in different parts of the pool. These apparently violent impacts did not deter either of them.

A great deal of nonsense has been written about otters both in captivity and in the wild, mostly by people who have never kept them successfully or have not studied them in their natural surroundings. I have seen it stated that otters will not use a chute unless the angle of incline is no more than so many degrees and the bottom of the chute actually enters the water. This is absurd, for otters will use almost anything as a slide provided the surface is slippery enough and the angle just sufficient for the force of gravity to work, and they certainly don't care if the end of the chute is in mid-air.

My friend H. G. Hurrel, the Devon naturalist, once kept two tame otters and I saw one of them repeatedly using a chute made of galvanized steel sheets, with evident enjoyment. The top of that chute was at least six feet high and to reach it the otter had to climb quite a steep step-ladder. Furthermore there was a drop of three feet from the end of the chute to the surface of the water.

Generally speaking I disapprove of animals in captivity being made to perform, but if an animal develops its own tricks and appears to enjoy them then I see no harm in encouraging it. This particularly applies to aquatic mammals, since otters, seals, sea-lions and dolphins are natural entertainers who, perhaps on account of their high level of intelligence, often invent their own repertoire of tricks, possibly to relieve the sheer boredom of captivity. Or perhaps like a dog they seek approbation from their keepers.

Common otters are believed to reach sexual maturity when about two years old and I waited impatiently for Gutsy and Ripple to grow up. They had occupied the enclosure in the Park for nearly two years when I went to India to make a film about the vanishing wildlife of the sub-continent. We were away three months and returned home in June.

As soon as we got back, I walked round the Park to see how all the animals looked. It was a beautiful, warm summer's evening, though it felt cool to me after the searing heat of

Central India. Turtle doves crooned monotonously, a thrush sang from the top of a full-leaved oak, its notes faintly echoed by a distant rival. Everything was green and lush, the air sweet with the scent of fresh-mown grass.

I came to the otters and they both swam across their pool to greet me, Gutsy rolling over on his back to grasp the end of my shooting stick with his fore-paws. I ran along the bank towing him to and fro, until he tired of the game. This is still one of his favourite pastimes and has become an evening ritual.

When they both came ashore I was immediately conscious of a change in Ripple; her belly sagged, and without a shadow of doubt she was pregnant.

Next morning Roy confirmed my opinion and we moved her to one of the maternity pens.

It is never easy to discern pregnancy in a common otter, particularly if one is in daily contact with the animal.

Two weeks later Ripple had her cubs. We could hear them clearly, squeaking inside her den. Once again I broke the rules and took a quick peep. Ripple lay curled up in her nest, two tiny cubs at her flank. They were about four inches long including their tails and were covered with pale grey, almost white, short fur.

Since this was the first time the Eurasian otter had been bred in captivity in Britain during the present century, I decided to make regular observations. When the cubs were just over two weeks old their fur changed to a darker grey, their eyes were still closed and they were just able to crawl but not to walk properly. The first youngster opened its eyes when thirty-one days old and the second three days later.

When they were thirty-six days old we decided to weigh them. To do this we had to drive Ripple out of the den without allowing her to drag a cub with her. They were a pair and the male weighed 22¾ ounces and the female two ounces lighter. I remember that their weights seemed light at the time, but this race of the Eurasian otter is smaller than our native animal. Even so, males would undoubtedly have weighed more.

I kept a daily watch on the babies' progress and saw them eat some solid food for the first time when they were seven weeks old. Three weeks later they regularly shared their mother's dinner, although I frequently saw her suckling them and by then they were active and able to run about.

One of the things I particularly wanted to see was the cubs' first introduction to water and in this I was lucky. It was my usual practice to keep watch as dusk approached, for this was the time when they were most active. One evening early in October, Ripple emerged from her den, sniffed the air, yawned a couple of times then saw me and 'huffed'. She ran across to the gate where I was sitting as if to make sure it was only me and 'huffed' again before moving over to her food bowl.

The cubs, then three months old, soon joined her and after taking a few mouthfuls began to play, chasing each other round the enclosure and indulging in bouts of wrestling in which the object appeared to be to floor one's opponent then, crouching over her, try to bite her throat. It looked rough and was accompanied by a good deal of puffing and panting but neither seriously hurt the other. When they were temporarily exhausted, one of them went back to Ripple, but the other approached the edge of the pool and, after hesitating, hung over the side and put its head briefly beneath the surface; it then slid down into the water and bobbing like a cork swam unsteadily round in a half circle before climbing out again. Ripple was less than ten yards away and fully aware of what was happening, but she took no notice of her cub's activities and certainly made no attempt either to encourage it to swim or to rescue it.

I am certain this was the cubs' first swim for I had watched them regularly during the preceding weeks and had seen them lean over the pool to drink quite often, but they had always taken care not to lean too far in case they lost their balance. Moreover, I always examined their tracks in the sand round the pool in the morning and had seen no evidence that either of them had been in before. This confirmed my belief that female otters do not often have to teach their cubs to swim, or even to encourage them to enter water unless circumstances are such that the cubs are compelled to go in much earlier than usual.

We weighed the youngsters again when they were eleven weeks old; the larger turned the scales at 35 ounces and her sister at 25⅞ ounces.

When they were six months old, it was clear that Ripple was getting fed up with them, which wasn't surprising since the bigger cub often squabbled with her at feeding times and had twice bitten her above the eye, causing a nasty swelling which only subsided when we gave her antibiotics in her food. The time had come for the family to be split up, so we moved the cubs, whom we had christened Rhona and Rhum, to another enclosure which they shared with a young male. Ripple rejoined Gutsy who was plainly delighted to see her back. The moment she was let out of the crate he ran up 'whickering' with excitement and kissed her face and head. Ripple took the rather boisterous welcome calmly and made her way to the pool where they both went through their routine of diving, rolling, swimming on their backs and corkscrewing through the water with that supple, effortless grace which makes otters, in their natural element, so enchanting to watch. From time to time Gutsy made half-hearted attempts to mate by clinging on Ripple's back and seizing the nape of her neck in his mouth as she swam; she always dislodged him quite easily by diving or spinning on to her back.

4. Fury

About this time coypus had reached pest proportions on the waterways of Norfolk. Originally introduced from South America by fur farmers, this amiable rodent had established itself in the wild by the end of the Second World War when its fur, called nutria, had become unfashionable. Some had doubtless escaped from fur farms, others had been set free when the market for their skins dried up, and in the broads and marshes of Norfolk they found a paradise and quickly multiplied. The coypu is a comparatively harmless, slow-moving, gentle vegetarian and although more closely related to the beaver than to the rat, he is more often linked to the latter on account of his naked rat-like tail. Furthermore most people find his prominent, brilliant orange incisor teeth somewhat repellent – poor animal, if only he listened to the TV advertisements and used the right toothpaste.

The coypu's main trouble, apart from a taste for sugar beet, is that he is apt to damage the banks of river, broad and canal. It's not that he indulges in a complicated labyrinth of burrows, but rather that he continually digs away at the water's edge and plays havoc with the reed beds and the aquatic vegetation.

When their numbers became unacceptable the Ministry of Agriculture organized a small army of trappers equipped with vans and thousands of traps in the hope of wiping out this alien invader. The traps were wire cages working on the same principle as the box mouse trap. Baited with apple, turnip or sugar beet they were placed in runs or paths near water and the poor old coypu, thankful for an easy meal, blundered in and was caught. In the morning the trapper on his rounds despatched the captive with a ·22 rifle bullet and sold its skin.

News had reached me that coypus were not the only animals being caught, shot and sold for their fur. Apparently, and for no explicable reason, otters occasionally entered the traps to suffer the same fate. Their pelts were worth a good deal more.

On hearing this, I got in touch with the officials in charge of the trapping operation and with as many trappers as possible and told them all I would pay five pounds for every otter alive and unharmed. Over the following three years eight otters came to me in this way. I released six of them locally on a stretch of the River Wensum where I knew they would be comparatively safe, since the farmers were friends of mine and did not allow the otter hounds on their land. Two I kept, Ginger and another female whom I called Whitelips because of the amount of white round her muzzle and on her chin.

When Ripple's cubs were about fourteen weeks old I began to suspect that Ginger might be pregnant. We moved her to an empty maternity pen. I looked at her daily, hoping to see more obvious signs of a coming event, but alas, no change was detectable. The staff began to pull my leg and more out of bravado than anything else, I said I was sure I was right and time would tell. Time did, for four weeks later one of the girls was scrubbing out Ginger's pool when she heard quite distinctly the squeaking of newborn cubs coming from the hut. This time I determined to take no risks and steeled myself to resist the temptation to have a quick peek. Every day I enquired whether anyone had heard the cubs whimpering and when nobody had, I was convinced things had gone wrong. A week passed and I could bear the suspense no longer. I slid back the lid of the den and peered inside. Ginger flew at me swearing and as she moved I saw she had a cub – just one and a big one at that.

We left her alone until the cub was twelve days old, by which time it could crawl about quite actively. Having shut Ginger out, I took the opportunity to fix a microphone in one corner of the hut just beneath the lid and with the help of George, our maintenance man, ran an overhead cable on poles the two hundred yards to our sitting-room.

For the next few weeks I kept a listening watch every evening from about nine o'clock until midnight and sometimes later.

The microphone was so sensitive I could hear Ginger breathing if I turned up the level sufficiently. Whenever she moved, the cub squealed loudly, especially when she left it and went outside to eat; then I could hear her jaws champing away in the background and the splash and lap of water when she went for a swim. Upon her return the cub squealed louder than ever and she huffed and chattered back, a very low confidential note.

One could clearly hear the cub suckling; this normally occurred once during the evening listening spell. Sometimes it indulged in further brief bouts of feeding but never for long. As time passed the cub became more silent and after its eyes opened, at thirty-three days of age, it squeaked only rarely when Ginger left it. All in all, life inside an otter's holt must be as silent and secretive as the animal's nocturnal habits suggest.

We christened the cub Gobble and he grew apace, weighing 2 lb. 5½ oz. when thirty-six days old.

One of my tamest otters was found one gale-swept night abandoned as a small cub beside a highland burn and taken to Mrs Innocent on the Isle of Mull. She has described for me, in her own words, the trials of rearing a baby otter.

'Joy and Terry arrived about 11.30 a.m. carrying a carton and wishing me a happy birthday (in advance). When I peered into the box there was an animal looking like an aggressive mongoose who had been out all night in the gale. It was an otter cub – I transferred her to a tea chest lined with newspaper and hay – I did this by tipping the box she was in into the tea chest, so did not handle her.

'After everyone had left (about two hours), I went quietly into the room and sat for some considerable time talking to her – and then, putting on leather gloves, slowly tried to accustom her to my efforts to touch her. It was thus that she was named Fury; there was really no other choice. She spat, screeched and flew at the gloved hands – as I had to handle her it seemed pointless to withdraw and so I picked up the terrified squeaking bundle of rage and realized how little I knew about young otters. On puppy experience I put her age between six and nine weeks but it was pure guess-work. Not expecting very much I tried her with evaporated milk very slightly diluted; it was of course a pointless occupation and after spending five minutes trying to form some kind of relationship, I returned her to the warmth, comparative safety and darkness of her box – I then sat down to consider the whole problem.

'Here was a cub over the age of imprint, and semi-dependent; she had been found by Neil and Keith, by the Fank gate, transported, by tail, box and hand to Croig where she had been laid on the ground, nosed by wellington boots and put several times in shallow water – not an ideal beginning. Of course I had several books on otters; none gave information on diets, housing, etc.; all seemed to have completely ignored this stage of adjustment to humans. I then rang up the local doctor who has had some success with birds and small mammals, but who, apart from his insistence on bottle-feeding (in which I had little confidence), was not able to help in this case. Nevertheless as Fury's next handling time approached I prepared a bottle for her – about one tablespoonful of evaporated milk.

'I might have saved myself the trouble. There was certainly no problem getting the teat into her mouth as she was screaming with rage at the whole frightening indignity of the performance. She worried the teat like a terrier a rat and with one twist of the head had the teat off, then herself, the room, and me spattered with milk. I may say that, against my better judgement, but in view of everybody's consolidated advice (caused mainly by the wide variants of opinion on her age – from four weeks to four months) we went through this performance again at the next feeding time, which did very little to further any good relationship between Fury and me.

'In the afternoon we were visited by several people wishing to see Fury and offering well-meaning but useless advice; it was either that day or the next morning that I decided that, in order to adapt to people, Fury would be better if she could not escape from the sights and noises of living, which she was doing by being kept in a tea chest. So we brought up the rabbit run, put it alongside one wall of the living-room, and in it I placed a sawn-in-two tea chest with a lid which I kept off for certain periods. Paper was put on the floor for warmth and cleanliness and also an earth box.

'By this time I was beginning to worry about her refusal to look at food, and realized that it was not physical difficulty – considering what she had been through she was a remarkably healthy little otter – but a rebellion against this alien world into which she had been plunged. At the next feed I offered her a variety of sardines, rabbit and minced beef. She made a tentative move towards the rabbit and did take one small piece, but she appeared to mouth it indifferently and out it came again – I tried dropping it into her bed, but if she saw or heard it she either spat with fear or ignored it.

'She was at last getting a little more resigned to being handled, and the fight before taking her out of the box was less prolonged. So far I could not consider what she should be eating, only what she could be induced to take. Finally at night, she did take a very little evaporated milk, with great difficulty and with a suck not a lap, but I judged she had had one tablespoonful. At this time I also noted that because of the tension in her it was impossible to pick her up by the scruff. She was capable of making this a rigid line of muscle on which you could get no hold; she also exuded a musk-like scent when handled as a skunk does. I left her for the night with various varieties of food and an untippable small bowl of water.

'My sitting-room, where she was, connects with my attic bedroom by ladder, so I knew I should hear her if I were needed. I was needed and useless all night – Fury spent the whole night whistling on every variation of note, a heart-breaking call for the bitch otter, so much so that at 2 a.m. I took myself up the hill near a small burn at the entrance of which Fury had been found, hoping I might hear an adult otter whistling and might somehow get the two together, but after three-quarters of an hour I realized this was not going to be the answer to our problems. The next day we went through the same mealtime performances. By now I was really worried, wondering, as one always does, whether it would have been kinder to have left her in her natural environment; but I still think the chances of her surviving would have been pretty small. We had now tried, without success, scraped beef, sardine, cooked rabbit, live eel (which I dropped in front of her hoping there would be a natural reaction which would start her eating; there wasn't) and she was existing on a very small quantity of slightly diluted evaporated milk with glucose. Benjie decided to try and contact some known authority on otters. In the meantime I was down in the harbour trying to catch eels, thank goodness it was spring tides. I found about fifty and managed to catch five which I brought home in a bucket of sludge, stones, and sea water. The lobster boys, who were very concerned, arrived with ten cockles – I cooked these by just dropping them into boiling water and taking them out again. I took Fury, who was now more resigned to this procedure, and offered her a cockle in my gloved hand. She grabbed it voraciously, mouthed it, but seemed to have great difficulty in actually masticating. At once I cut up six of them with scissors and put them in a bowl which I held for her, and blessed relief, she took the lot. I could have leapt over the moon, she had obviously reached the point where, for food at least, she was prepared to co-operate . . .

'I had decided the run was a great mistake – she needed the rest and security of the tea chest, and I had returned her to it. This was on Thursday, and when Benjie returned from her phone call to London Zoo armed with information, it was cheering to find I had done nothing too dreadful, but awesome to envisage the difficulties ahead if Fury were to survive. The first stumbling block, which has proved insurmountable, was the recommended temperature "an even 75°". Our lives are primitive and limited financially, so we burn for the most part peat and wood, which you can get here. So I had to settle for 60° which nearly killed me, but I'd manage anyhow until it got colder. She was to have ABDEC (vitamin drops) in addition to the halibut oil, which I had already given, also calcium and bone meal. But first we had to get her eating and eels were greatly recommended; however we were now back on the neap tides so that source was closed for another ten days.

'We were told that the cub was probably about eight weeks old on the day after we had weighed it, at which time she (still unsexed) was just 2 lb. The rest of the information was very depressing. The dangers of diarrhoea and pneumonia hung over me. At the next feed she took her milk much more adeptly. Thank goodness I had never contemplated cow's milk, which appears to be fatal, and she had had a motion, dark and oily. She was more amenable to being picked up but very unpredictable, and susceptible to light, ducking and hissing at moving shadows. I had been advised to feed her hourly, but I felt this would give her no rest at all, and settled for three-hourly.

'Fury had cockles, evaporated milk, and oysters as her main diet. In the evening I cooked the eels, chopped them up very small and they were taken without any trouble. At every meal I tried her on raw scraped beef and she occasionally took a very little, which worried me as I knew with the change of tides we should no longer be able to get shellfish. And anybody who has lived in the islands knows that real fish is like gold. During this time I found out how personally clean she was which added to the responsibility one had towards her, as she frequently whistled and cried between feeds to be let out to use her lavatory (an old dog rug under the angle of the ladder).'

As Fury grew she naturally became much more active and needed more space than the croft could provide. Reluctantly, Mrs Innocent had to find a new home for her and quite by chance, she heard of our success with breeding otters and decided to write to me. I knew how she must feel at the prospect of parting with little Fury upon whom she had lavished so much loving care. Against all odds, she had reared the foundling, and in her way, Fury had responded and returned her affection.

Despite their rather solitary existence in the wild, otters become very strongly attached to their human foster parents and will not easily transfer their affections to a new owner. I could imagine Fury's misery had she been sent off to a zoo where nobody would have had the time or the inclination to play with her and try to lessen her grief by offering friendship and security such as she had known.

From our point of view, Fury's arrival was a godsend since British otters are very hard to come by, and here was another potential breeding female to add to our group, who one day perhaps would make a positive contribution to my dream of reintroducing captive-bred otters to suitable wildlife reserves in this country, and so help to ensure the continued survival of the most enchanting of all our wild mammals.

One bleak November day, a rather frightened Fury arrived at Great Witchingham. She brought her treasured possessions with her, an old piece of sheepskin, a woolly ball and a toy penguin with bells inside it, which tinkled whenever it was moved. Knowing Fury had been kept inside the warm croft, we had prepared a large shed for her. It had a wooden floor and insulated walls, but plenty of light from windows in the roof. In one corner, we fixed a sleeping box full of hay, over which we suspended an infra-red lamp to keep the bed warm and dry. The floor was covered with a deep layer of sand, and at one end we put a large shallow trough of water.

Unlike our other otters, Fury had not been accustomed to swimming and I felt it better to keep her inside until the weather turned warmer and to acclimatize her gradually to life in a large open pen. She seemed to like her new hut, especially the warm bed into which she immediately dragged her beloved piece of sheepskin. Clearly this was her favourite thing, and she always slept underneath it, even after she had dragged it through her bath and it was soaking wet. When Mrs Innocent's friend who brought her left, Fury whistled in despair, but Barbara, one of our staff, took over and spent many hours coaxing and consoling her.

Just as I had been told, Fury was a friendly and playful little creature, always welcoming anyone who went to see her by running to the door squealing with pleasure. Although she allowed me to pick her up when she first arrived, it was obvious that she felt more confident with women and she took to Barbara straight away, jumping into her lap within a few days and permitting herself to be carried into the warm room where the staff have their lunch. There she played around on the floor while they ate their meal, chasing her toy penguin which she always retrieved for Barbara, but no one else.

For Fury it was a new and fascinating world to be explored – buckets to overturn, piles of sacks in which to burrow and since she was adept at climbing, all manner of things to knock off the table, which she reached by way of a chair. Sometimes she jumped on to one of the men's laps and very often nipped him, but she never bit the girls, and Barbara could pick her up by the base of her tail and carry her in her arms like a baby. The toy penguin became very useful as a lure, for Fury would come running to the sound of its tinkling bells.

I felt she might be difficult over the change in her diet, but she quickly adapted to dead day-old chicks, for which she developed a passion, and to a variety of fresh fish, though she took longer to get on to our standard otter mix, which may be an acquired taste.

As the weather improved, Barbara began to take her outside for walks, gradually increasing the distance until their daily excursions included a stroll in the Park. I always felt that, surrounded by the perimeter fence, this was the safest place, since Fury couldn't possibly run away. I am sure now that I worried unnecessarily, for she never showed the slightest inclination to leave Barbara for long, though she was always ready to play her up. Sometimes she ran into the belt of trees not far from the Park gate and hid in the undergrowth or disappeared beneath one of the wooden brooder huts and refused to come out.

As with all otters, there was only one way to respond to pranks and that was to wait patiently until she lost interest in whatever she was doing and began to feel lonely. Then, and only then, would she come scampering back to the sound of the penguin's bells.

Otters vary as much in temperament as people and Fury soon began to display her peculiar traits. That she became a 'one girl' otter imprinted on, or perhaps more accurately, attached to Barbara was not unexpected, but Fury carried this alliance a stage further, for she allowed Barbara to pick her up and take away her food when she was eating. Not many carnivores will permit such liberties.

Unlike most otters, Fury never chased birds in the Park, except in a sense of fun and not once has she made a serious attempt to kill even a pinioned duck which, flapping and somersaulting across the grass, is more than most otters can resist. On the other hand, retrieving has always been Fury's forte and with little encouragement she began to bring back dead day-old chicks for Barbara like a Labrador with a dummy bird.

Fury was a self-taught swimmer; because of her upbringing she learned this skill rather late in life, being about nine months old before she really mastered it. Just below the seal pond in the Park lies a small shallow pond much frequented by our flock of barnacle geese. Fury often passed this way on her daily round and sometimes she enjoyed herself by rushing playfully at the geese, scattering them in honking wing-flapping panic, then turning back to explore the pond. At first she stuck to the bank, merely putting her head into the muddy water, but gradually she began to paddle until she was swimming with her front paws, while keeping her hind feet firmly on the bottom.

Then one day she took the plunge and became water-borne. After that there was no stopping her, as she porpoised and dived in the muddy depths, her small rudder breaking surface from time to time to mark her course.

As Fury grew up, she lost interest in her penguin toy, which in any case had not withstood the ravages of time, so Barbara removed the bells from the woollen cadaver and tied them on to a new piece of string. When she felt inclined, Fury still came running to their sound.

All in all, I think she enjoyed her new life, especially with the advent of summer which meant more freedom for her as she often accompanied Barbara while she carried on with her daily work in the Park. At lunchtime they joined the rest of the staff, sitting out in the sun when Fury, inquisitive as ever, examined the contents of everybody's lunch box.

5. Kate and Lucy

My first experience of rearing otter cubs was with Ginger's second litter. She had given birth to two youngsters exactly twenty-eight days earlier, when I asked Roy to weigh them. This he did, and reported that both were females weighing 1 lb. 10 oz. and 1 lb. 10½ oz. respectively. They were in excellent condition and their eyes were tiny slits, just beginning to open. While the cubs were being handled Ginger played and swam in her pool, returning to her den as the men were leaving her enclosure. Roy remarked how sleek and fit she looked.

Two hours later I happened to pass that way and to my horror found Ginger lying panting and half-drowned in the shallows, her hind legs trailing and obviously paralysed. Running back to the barn I collected a catching net and returned to the pool with two of the staff. We quickly lifted Ginger from the water and put her back with her cubs in the den, but my worst fears were confirmed, for she was quite unable to move her hind quarters which trailed helplessly behind her as she dragged herself along with her front paws. When the vet arrived he gave her broad spectrum antibiotics as well as injections for milk-fever and we transferred her to a deep bed of dry straw in a heated compartment of the sick quarters. There she lay under an infra-red lamp quite unable to communicate to us the intensity of her pain or the depth of her grief for her lost cubs. That night she ate little and the following day we took her down to the surgery for an X-ray which showed little beyond two calcified vertebrae which might have been responsible for her paralysis.

Meanwhile my wife was patiently feeding the two baby otters on Ostermilk mixed slightly stronger than the proportion recommended for human babies. She began with a small pipette but next day changed to an ordinary baby's bottle which the cubs much preferred. She fed them every five hours starting at 7 a.m. and giving them their last feed at 10.30 p.m. For the first few days they each took just under one ounce of the mixture at every feed, but two weeks later they were knocking back two and a half ounces each at every feed. They grew stronger daily and as their eyes opened they became much more active and it was necessary to give them periods of exercise by allowing them to crawl about on a dust-sheet spread out on the living-room carpet. At night and between feeds they slept in a deep cardboard box lined with newspaper and kept near a warm radiator.

After every feed I put each in turn on the draining board, and holding its tail in my left hand, dangled its rear end over the sink while I massaged its anal region with a wad of warm wet cotton-wool. This nearly always induced the cub to relieve itself and, after a quick dry on a towel, it was put back with its sister.

Although Ginger made some progress, she failed to recover, and died six months later. The post-mortem revealed that her paralysis had indeed been caused by the two fused vertebrae.

The two babies, whom we christened Lucy and Kate, were the most attractive animals I have ever had. Their wide flat noses and tiny blue-grey eyes gave them a permanently doleful expression, and after a good feed, their little tummies distended with milk, they resembled two small brown Buddhas. As their legs grew stronger so did their voices and while one was being fed, interrupting bouts of noisy sucking with querulous chirruping like a small bird, the other, left alone in the box, uttered ear-piercing shrieks on a single note similar to the adult otter's famous 'whistle'.

As they grew bigger, they made repeated attempts to climb out of their cardboard nursery, until one of them finally scrabbled to the top, balanced uneasily on the edge for a second, then nose-dived on to the carpet. Fearing they would climb out in the night and get cold we transferred them to a small otter's travelling box made of plywood with a wire-mesh front. This we lined with sheets of newspaper changed at each feed, and put beside a radiator in the kitchen.

When they were six weeks old, the cubs were taking five ounces of the mixture between them at each feed, five times a day, but sometimes they were not hungry so we soon reduced the number of feeds to four daily. While still unsteady on their hind legs, they were able to run quite well, and after each feed we put them on the lawn for a bout of exercise. Squeaking loudly they ran after us, side by side, like a pair of animated fur gloves bumping into each other and tumbling over in their frenzy not to get left behind. Sometimes I ran away from them and as soon as they lost contact they became disorientated, tottering round in circles, squeaking. If I stood quite still about ten feet away they could not see me though the moment I called they came running to nuzzle at my ankles.

Mothering played an important part in their lives and if they were temperamental over their food, half an hour of fondling and playing on the drawing-room sofa often got them feeding again. Physical contact seemed to restore their confidence and sense of security. At this age each had developed her own character. Kate was much more independent than Lucy and less affectionate, but she learned more quickly. Having fallen nose first down the kitchen step once, she refused to go near it again, while Lucy was always ready to launch herself into space regardless of the drop. Kate had a quicker temper and was inclined to be more aggressive, sometimes taking it out on her slightly smaller sister.

We were not looking forward to weaning the babies, but at seven weeks old they began to get bored with their milk and it was obvious they needed something more substantial. With some misgiving I filleted a raw herring and chopped it up finely. Taking hold of Lucy I opened her mouth, put a morsel of fish on her tongue, and to my surprise she champed it with a good deal of noise and evident enjoyment. Soon she was eating from the saucer and all I had to do was to keep pushing the fish into a little pile with one finger so she could pick it up more easily. Kate took longer to adjust to the new method of feeding, but once hooked on fish they both quickly lost all interest in milk.

Thereafter we fed them three times daily on chopped fresh haddock with a raw egg on it and occasionally herring. At first they refused our canned carnivore food made by Spratts which all adult otters seem to like, but gradually they accepted it, mixed with fish and a pinch of vitamin and mineral supplement.

When the weather was fine, we put them outside on the lawn in a glorified baby's playpen made of wood and wire netting, though they still spent the night by the kitchen radiator. After their last feed I always took them on to the lawn where they both relieved themselves before being put to bed. If the weather happened to be windy and wet they lost no time in performing this function, immediately rushing back to the kitchen door.

After each meal we washed their faces and front paws, which they always pushed into their food, under the kitchen tap before drying them on a warm towel. They loved this and it was perhaps the highlight of their day. They snuggled down into the soft folds and lay still and limp while being rubbed and fondled. Next came a drink of water and we found the easiest way to administer this was out of a mug, since one could hold it firmly by the handle while the otter plunged its head inside to drink, which it did with a great deal of sucking and gurgling.

Lucy was a much tidier feeder than Kate and she drank with more finesse – until she had had enough – then suddenly she would dip her head into the water and blow hard, sending a cold spray all over us and the kitchen.

We decided to weigh the cubs every month until they were mature, and to do this each was put in a small linen bag and placed on the scales. At eight weeks Kate weighed 2 lb. 7 oz. and Lucy 2 lb. 5 oz. so we felt they were growing as fast as they would have done had Ginger brought them up.

They often had the run of the house and on the whole did surprisingly little damage. True, Lucy once scampered into the hall and disappeared beneath the old oak kist. There she discovered with evident joy that the bottom was covered with some sort of ancient fabric and that the height was such that lying on her back, she could brace herself with her paws while stripping layers of the material with her teeth.

The cubs, always highly strung, found the kitchen boiler a safe retreat the moment anything frightened them, for there was just sufficient room to squeeze behind it and lurk out of sight between the outer cover and the actual boiler. It must have been warm and snug and was, without doubt, their favourite place, from which it was often infuriatingly difficult to entice them. There was no question of pulling them out since no human hand and arm could follow the otters' sinuous movements between the various pipes. After a lot of waiting and calling, a flat head might appear, bewhiskered with fluff and dust and smelling strongly of paraffin, only to draw back the moment one made a movement. The only time we had the laugh on the cubs and the boiler was when someone left the back door open months later when Kate was more than half-grown. Seeing her chance, she rushed from the garden into the kitchen, hesitated, then seemed to remember her beloved boiler: scampering across the room she dived behind it, only to get firmly wedged with little more than her head and shoulders safely out of sight.

As the cubs grew, they naturally made much more mess and alas, not always in their night hutches, for the coconut mat inside the back door appeared to be quite irresistible and from it there soon emanated a powerful odour which permeated the whole house. At this time Kate suddenly acquired the curious habit of relieving herself in the middle of the living-room sofa or in one of the armchairs, to such an extent that a guest arriving for dinner and observing a total lack of loose covers, which were all at the cleaners, remarked that presumably the name 'Kate' was short for 'defecate'. I particularly remember one evening when I sat down on the sofa to work on this book and immediately became conscious of a cold, wet and sticky seat. Cursing Kate, I removed a very smelly pair of trousers and put them with the loose cover from the cushion into the washing machine. Moving in my underpants to one of the chairs, I discovered too late that Kate had beaten me to it. My wife came in to find me sitting writing in the one usable chair clad only in a shirt and socks. As I expected, she told me Kate and Lucy had outstayed their welcome as house guests and that I must make other and more permanent arrangements for them.

We had made the small garden at the front of our cottage otter-proof, and had provided a pool on the lawn, but these quarters were already occupied by our tame pair of Asian short-clawed otters, Freckie and her husband Kuala – so named because he had been bred in the Zoo at Kuala Lumpur. It seemed a pity to move them from their established home and territory. Furthermore, the tiny Asian short-clawed otter is no digger and therefore relatively harmless in a garden, whereas a full-grown European otter can dig a sizeable burrow in a single night if it feels so inclined.

There was no alternative but to dig another pond to the rear of the house and provide Kate and Lucy with a large enclosure, complete with a sturdy shed and, at any rate for their first winter, an infra-red heater over their bed. They seemed to enjoy their new life, probably because they could swim whenever they wanted to.

At about this time we stopped robbing our deep-freeze cabinet and weaned them from their favourite food of filleted haddock and raw egg on to the regular diet of otter mix, herring and eels. Once they got used to them, eels became their favourite dish, as they are with most otters.

It was soon noticeable that the cubs' daily activity followed a fairly regular pattern and corresponded to the routine of adult otters that I had previously observed. They were most active in the evening from about an hour before dusk to around midnight. Thereafter, they usually slept until about an hour before dawn, when they again became very busy until well after the sun was up.

I remember feeling slightly guilty when we first put Kate and Lucy into their new enclosure. I felt we were robbing them of their liberty and that even their new pool was a poor substitute for the freedom they had previously enjoyed. Looking back, I'm sure the situation worried me much more than it worried the otters, for they soon became strongly attachcd to their new home, and if woken in the middle of the day and called out they sometimes refused to move, preferring to lie on their backs under the warmth of the lamp, yawning and stretching. The evening was a different matter: then they both stood up at the wire netting fence squeaking loudly to be let out and taken for a walk.

The evening walk round the Park gradually became an established pattern in their lives and in ours and has remained so to this day. At first, they followed very close to our heels squealing with fear at getting left behind and soon tiring, so that often we carried them a little way before putting them down again. They quickly felt the heat on a warm summer night and would lie panting until we picked them up. As they grew stronger, they became more venturesome and began to investigate all the new objects they encountered. Whenever possible, litter bins had to be overturned and the contents spread, while clumps of bushes became in their minds jungles to be explored.

Lucy was especially keen on feathers, particularly white ones which, if found, she would pounce on and carry triumphantly in her mouth. Always the more extrovert and apparently fearless, she was the leader while Kate, already a good deal bigger and heavier, pottered along behind her, always ready to run back to us the moment anything strange frightened her.

Now four months old, their eyesight had improved enormously and they could distinguish either of us from strangers at twenty yards. When we had first taken them out in the Park a month earlier, they had had difficulty in locating us in the open at anything over six yards and only found us by ear if we called at regular intervals. Their hearing was always highly sensitive and they were able to detect sounds quite inaudible to our ears. Hearing is obviously extremely important to such a nocturnal and secretive animal and gradually we began to understand the cubs' language. The ultra high-pitched squeak

– sometimes euphemistically referred to as a whistle – is essentially a contact call: 'I'm here, where are you?'

As might be expected, strange sounds were far more fearful to the young otters than new shapes and perhaps the most frightening of all was the noise of a tractor. The grass in the Park has to be cut during the long summer evenings when there are no visitors and we use a large mower pulled by a tractor. The noise of its engine frightened the cubs more than anything else – so much so that it was useless to attempt to take them anywhere near it. It is said that real fear experienced in childhood leaves an unhealing scar and it was certainly true in Kate and Lucy's case. When they were very small cubs, we used to let them out of their play-pen to roam in the garden, and on one particular morning they were playing hide-and-seek in the hedge when the old gardener went by with a motor mower. At its approach the cubs froze with fear; oblivious, Fred went ahead. At that moment my wife realized what was happening and shouted to warn him that the cubs were out. Unable to hear her above the racket of the engine, he stopped almost on top of Kate and Lucy – the damage to their nerves had been done.

At the Max Planck Institute in Bavaria, Konrad Lorenz has shown how goslings become imprinted on the first moving object they see after breaking out of the egg. In the wild, this is always their parents, but in captivity a bantam or a human is just as acceptable. He has further shown that they can recognize a distinctive pattern on their human foster parent's wellingtons and learn to follow them.

The first moving objects which Kate and Lucy saw on opening their eyes were my wife and me, so it is not surprising that they became imprinted on us. In the early days she fed them more often than I did, so if anything, they were more attached to her. But now we were taking them for walks a new pattern of behaviour emerged, for if we both took them out Lucy nearly always followed Jeanne's heels while Kate kept close behind me. They made their own choice and have kept to it ever since, though to a certain extent we are interchangeable and they will follow either of us when we are alone.

During the winter Jeanne often wore bright red wellingtons which both cubs soon learnt to recognize, though like nearly all mammals, otters see in monochrome. At the start of a walk they often jumped up to nip her legs just above her boots and for quite a long time we were at a loss to understand the reason. Then we realized they wanted to be picked up and fondled. If she was out alone with them and carried one cub, the other immediately became jealous and bit her legs quite hard. Curiously enough they never attempted to nip me, though they jumped up when they wanted a lift.

The cubs' daily walk presented problems when we went away. We felt it reasonable to leave them in their enclosure for a night or two, but not for longer periods, so when we decided to have a short holiday on the west coast of Scotland other arrangements had to be made, and a fortnight before our departure we began to train a young member of our staff to take over. For three or four nights he accompanied us with Kate and Lucy who, after initial suspicion, soon began to ignore him. At length they even approached him, but they only allowed him to stroke them if one of us was holding them. They made it very clear that any attempt on his part to pick up either of them would result in a serious bite. After a week or so they reluctantly followed him round the Park provided neither of us were present and only if he stuck exactly to their accustomed route. By the time we went away we felt that Antony would be able to cope and could get them back into their pen with the aid of a few eels.

The first night things went well enough, except that they played him up for over half an hour when he tried to put them to bed. The next night they were bent on mischief and half-way round the Park both ran off and hid in a thick belt of young fir trees. They had done exactly the same thing to me on several occasions and sometimes I'd waited an hour before they decided to come out. At intervals and especially if I stopped calling, a brown head would pop out through the long grass at the edge of the trees to make sure I was still there, only to disappear again immediately. Sometimes I heard them rushing through the undergrowth in joyous chase of a moorhen or a baby rabbit. Once Lucy emerged triumphant with a dead fledgeling blackbird in her mouth, to be followed by Kate with another from the same brood a few moments later.

Of course both cubs knew my voice well enough and no doubt regarded my calls as a reassuring contact note. Antony did not have this advantage and they kept him waiting for two hours while they played amongst the trees and chased out every living thing.

As the light began to fade he became worried and started to walk back towards the farm with the idea of getting a net in which to attempt to catch them. To his astonishment he suddenly became aware of a dark shadow following a few yards behind. He sat down on the grass and Lucy approached and climbed on to his lap. On the principle that an otter in the hand was worth two in a wood, he bravely grabbed her only to be bitten through the base of his thumb. Despite this he hung on and made for home carrying Lucy under her arms as one lifts a child. She made no further attempt to bite and after putting her securely in her pen he returned to look for Kate, but the wood was silent in the gloaming and of Kate there was no sign.

The following morning he and Roy searched the Park, but found nothing apart from a pinioned wigeon which had been freshly killed and half eaten – Kate had obviously dined well during the night. Next day Roy noticed an otter's tracks in the fresh earth outside a rabbit burrow in a clump of gorse bushes and he and Antony set to work with spades and dug out the entire warren without finding Kate.

That night a curlew was killed in the wader pool as well as another duck so they knew Kate was still around, but nobody had any idea where to search for her until a visitor, chancing to look inside one of the shelters on the pheasant lawn, noticed an otter curled up asleep with a peacock for company sitting on the perch above. Roy and Antony were taking no chances and armed with two nets soon had a protesting Kate safely inside a travelling box and on her way to rejoin Lucy. That was the cubs' last walk until we returned.

As they grew they not only changed in appearance, Kate being larger and heavier in build, but in character as well. Lucy was still the extrovert, always curious and ready for new adventures. Compared with Kate she was utterly fearless and seemed to lack any instinctive wariness so long as humans were not involved, for both otters had an innate suspicion of strangers as they did of machines and other man-made objects.

Our usual round took us past the foxes' enclosure and Vicki, our tame vixen, always came to see me to nibble my fingers gently through the netting. This was invariably the signal for Lucy to rush at the wire huffing and chittering at the fox which tried to snap at her nose. Undaunted, Lucy then ran on past the fallow deer until she came to their gate where she was able to squeeze through the large mesh netting to besport herself, swimming in their water trough. One evening a curious doe put her nose down to examine this strange sight and Lucy immediately flew at her and nipped her. The doe drew back stamping the ground in anger, while the rest of the herd gathered round stamping with their front feet.

We were worried for Lucy's safety – she looked so tiny compared with the surrounding deer – but, in her own time, she crawled back through the gate and followed us. Her next escapade was to climb up the netting of the little owl's aviary and prance about on the roof, using it like a trampoline to the owl's evident consternation. This time Kate decided to join her sister and they were so engrossed in the new game that neither took any notice of our efforts to get them down until Lucy, intent on discovering something new, decided to follow us. She ran to the front of the aviary and fearlessly launched herself into space, dropping eight feet on to the grass below without coming to any harm.

When Kate reached the edge her nerve failed and she stopped, squeaking loudly for assistance. Running back, I stretched up only to find she was just beyond my grasp. Kate, still squealing, hesitated, then hanging on with every claw in her hind feet and trembling with fear, lowered herself over the edge, her long body stretching like elastic, until I was just able to reach her shoulders and lift her down.

Of course there were certain animals we avoided as a safety precaution. One was the wolverine, whose enclosure, although having a dry moat six feet deep on the inside, was surrounded on the outside by a wall only two feet high. Lucy was always attracted by the two wolverines as though she knew they were distant relatives, being the largest and fiercest members of the *Mustelidae*. We knew well enough what would happen should she decide on a closer acquaintance, so we tried to keep well away and always hurried past hoping she wouldn't notice while we diverted her attention.

The lynx enclosure was another danger-spot since Lucy would run up to the chain-link fence and taunt the cats who came to see her. Fortunately, she was just too fat to squeeze through the mesh, but a lynx could easily have put a paw through and seized her with dire results.

Our lynx enclosure is probably the largest in Europe, covering nearly three-quarters of an acre. About the size of an Alsatian dog, a lynx lying at the far side would be almost invisible, especially as there are trees and rocks behind which they can hide. To give visitors a fair chance of seeing them, we built a raised viewing point with only a low wall three feet high on the outside, but with a sheer drop of fifteen feet on the inside.

Most evenings we stopped, leaned on the wall and checked that all was well with the cats, while Kate and Lucy played around our feet. They soon became bored and scrabbled at our legs, squeaking to be lifted up so that they too could see over the parapet. Having had a good look, they were quite content to be put down again.

Perhaps there is a guardian angel who looks after curious and courageous little otters or maybe Kate and Lucy were just lucky, for only once was one of them injured as a result of their high spirits. It was getting dark and I was alone with them and heading back towards the house past the flamingo pool, when

Lucy suddenly climbed up the four-foot fence and dropped down on the inside closely followed by Kate. In the gathering darkness I could just see them rush down the bank into the water and then I could hear the commotion as the flamingoes cackled and honked, rushing and splashing in all directions, terrified by the two sinister objects torpedoing through the water of their pool. Remembering Kate's liking for curlew and ducks, I rushed into the pen and called to them without any success, nor could I see where they were except by the movement of the panic-stricken birds, for the cubs were happily herding them up and down the pool like a couple of sheep-dogs.

Giving up, I decided to return home and enlist Jeanne's help when Lucy, tiring of the flamingo hunt, came running after me. Gathering her in my arms I hurried back to the house and told Jeanne what had happened. She took Lucy to her pen while I returned to look for Kate.

By then it was really dark and when I got back to the pool I could just discern the flamingo flock herded at one end, while at the other I could see the ghostly white shapes of the pair of storks which live in the same enclosure. Suddenly the storks began to flap and rush about as Kate launched a submarine attack on one of them. Commotion quickly followed, the storks jumping and flapping their wings while stabbing at their hidden enemy with their dagger-sharp bills. A few moments later, Kate appeared at my feet and followed me obediently to the gate. Relieved that no damage had been done, I set off for home with the otter close by and on the way I sensed that her behaviour had changed. She seemed to be trying to keep as close to me as possible and twice I stopped and tried to pick her up, but each time she ran just out of reach. It was as if she realized she had been naughty and was demonstrating just how contrite an otter can be.

Jeanne met us on the lawn and I told her I felt there was something odd about Kate who, while keeping close to us, seemed loath to be picked up. In the end Jeanne caught her and carried her into the kitchen. As she walked into the bright light, I heard her gasp of horror, for the reason for Kate's behaviour was hideously clear. Her left eye was hanging out, having been removed by one deft stroke of the stork's scimitar bill. When we recovered from the shock we realized that the eye itself was still intact and although blood red, apparently not stabbed.

While Jeanne wrapped Kate up in a dry towel I telephoned our vet who told me to bring her to his surgery straight away. On the journey to Reepham, Kate lay quietly across my lap. After a careful examination and much to my relief, John said he could probably put the eye back and that although she might lose her sight in that eye, she would look quite normal. I put Kate on the operating table still wrapped in her towel and held my left hand over her mouth to prevent John being bitten. He worked the eye back into the socket as though he had done hundreds like it – which I am sure he hadn't. A hefty dose of antibiotics injected beneath her elastic skin and Kate, still wrapped in her warm towel, was once more on my lap and on the way home.

It was a cold night, so we decided to leave Kate in the kitchen in a box beside the boiler while she recovered from the shock. We gave her a bowl of water and a dish of her favourite baby food – haddock fillets covered with raw egg. She seemed exhausted and content to lie in the warmth of the familiar room. Leaving her, we went to bed.

Early next morning I got up and went downstairs to make the tea. On the way, I couldn't help wondering about Kate. Would she still be alive? Would her eye have stayed in position or would it have come out again? – something John had warned me might happen. As I approached the kitchen door, I was conscious of the sound of pop music. I opened the door and stood still, taking in the scene. Kate was up on the window-sill, apparently very lively and from a distance her eye looked normal. The kitchen was awash, the waste bucket on its side, its contents scattered, the dishes from the previous evening's meal lying on the floor, Jeanne's cookery books scattered in the mess and in the middle of it all, her portable radio lying on

1. Ripple with her cubs
Rhona and Rhum

2. Gutsy, father of the cubs

3. Gutsy in a playful mood

4. Kate and Lucy, 12 weeks old

5. Up to 6 weeks Kate and
Lucy slept in a cardboard box

6. Lucy and the eel that nearly got away

7. Kate and Lucy playing underwater

its side blaring out its early morning music. Kate, in her attempt to depart via the window, had climbed on top of it, pressing down the knob and had switched it on, before pushing it on to the floor.

Apart from being very bloodshot her eye soon recovered and moved normally in the socket, although she was unable to see with it. Gradually, as the blood dispersed, her sight improved and within a month appeared completely restored.

Certain places in the Park always induced the same behaviour on the part of the cubs, and one of these was a thicket of dogwood regularly used as a roost during the winter by hundreds of house sparrows. Fifty yards from the thicket the cubs charged off, crashing about in the undergrowth, flushing the sparrows in noisy fluttering hordes. They evidently enjoyed this routine immensely and never failed to carry it out.

Getting them back in their pen could be very tiresome, particularly as darkness approached and they became livelier and more excitable. Sometimes it was possible to grab one of them and put her away, hoping the other would follow, but as this rarely worked we developed a variety of ruses designed to catch them off their guard, when we could pick them up. Like small children, they disliked going to bed and ran off into the darkness or disappeared into the bracken and hid from us.

Occasionally they fell for a simple trick – but not if repeated too often. One of these was to pretend we were going for another walk by returning to the gate leading from our garden into the Park, calling to the cubs to come along quickly. If it worked they came scampering and stood up peering through the netting, waiting for the gate to be opened. A quick grab and if one was lucky, both cubs could be carried off to bed. If not, something else had to be tried.

Every third night all our otters had eels for dinner and then there was no problem, dangle an eel, chant 'eels, eels, eels' and they would follow you to the gates of hell. When all else had failed, we fell back on the last resort. Feigning total indifference, we came inside, being careful to leave the back door open. Such is their curiosity that this nearly always worked; besides, they still felt a strong attachment to the kitchen of their baby days. Once they were inside and occupied at the far end of the room, the outer door had to be swiftly closed. After that it was usually a simple matter to pick them up and carry them off.

This ruse was almost, but not quite, otter-proof, for both cubs never lost their love of a nice warm dry towel. Perhaps this was the most comforting thing they remembered from the time their eyes first opened on the world of people. Quite often one or other of them noticed the kitchen towel hanging from its hook near the sink and grabbing the end in its mouth, would dash madly out of the back door to hide with its spoil somewhere in the darkness outside. Usually the towels were only rediscovered months later, damp and dirty, in some unlikely spot.

The biggest problems always occurred when one of us was away and the other had to cope single-handed. Of course, Kate and Lucy took advantage of this heaven-sent opportunity to be really difficult. I cannot recall how many times I had one otter safely in the pen, spent ages trying to catch the other and at last succeeded, only to let the first one out again when trying to put her sister back. Jeanne relates how she went one better when on her own, for she finished up inside the enclosure with both otters outside peering at her through the netting squeaking with delight.

6. Otters in Camera

By this time I was seriously thinking of making a film about the life of the otter, since there seemed a reasonable chance that Ripple would breed again and so give me a unique opportunity to record an otter's complete life cycle. Quite by chance I discovered that Christopher Parsons of the BBC Natural History Unit at Bristol had been considering the same idea. After discussion it was decided that we should co-operate on the project and that the film would be made for the *World About Us* series of which Christopher was executive producer.

During the summer I designed a breeding den which was a replica of a natural holt, complete with tree roots and lined with waterside vegetation. The entire back consisted of a sheet of plate glass which could be raised silently by a nylon cord running over a pulley fixed beneath the roof of a darkened shed attached to the den. A curved burrow led from one of our breeding enclosures into the holt, making it dark and snug. Finally, I built a partition across the shed three feet from the glass with an opening in the centre for the camera lens. A photo-flood lamp was installed and carefully shielded, to give the effect of a shaft of light illuminating the centre of the holt. I was afraid that sudden light of this intensity might worry the otter so I incorporated a rheostat control on the rear wall of the shed so that illumination could be increased slowly according to the animals' reactions. A small pilot light was left on all the time to accustom the otter to some light in the holt.

Ripple obligingly became pregnant again, and separating her from Gutsy, we installed her in the breeding pen at the beginning of October. She took to the new holt immediately and I made a point of sitting inside the shed for an hour or so every day, talking to her quietly. Also I switched on the rheostat and accustomed her to an increasing amount of light. She took remarkably little notice apart from moving into the direct beam, where she lay and luxuriated in the warmth like a sun-seeker on a southern beach.

On the 22nd of the month she gave birth to two cubs. Though I saw them the next day, she seemed unsettled and I decided to leave her a little longer before commencing filming.

At the end of the week I set up the camera, switched on the rheostat and very cautiously raised the plate glass. This had to be done, since not only did it reflect the lamp, but I found it impossible to keep clean. Ripple became rather agitated at this manoeuvre but soon settled down, encircling her cubs tightly. I increased the light and for the very first time peered through the viewfinder to see an otter with her tiny pale grey, almost white, cubs looking as relaxed as they doubtless would in a riverside holt. Soothingly I called her name and she looked up and hugged her cubs more closely. I suddenly realized that Ripple had allowed me into the most secret part of an otter's world, and with luck some of those secrets would soon be on film to be enjoyed by millions.

I had to be content with occasional glimpses of the babies since Ripple took great care to hide them, often spending long periods asleep curled full-circle with her back to me, the cubs concealed beneath her interlocking fore and hind leg. Sometimes a strange sound outside the holt made her look up and then, if I was lucky, I could see them and had time to study their bright pink, almost raw-looking square-shaped muzzles, their tiny pink ear orifices and miniature salmon-pink pads. Such moments were all too brief, and so small were the cubs that Ripple could easily conceal one of them beneath a front paw as she clasped it to her flank.

Whenever she moved, the cubs began to chirrup softly and sometimes I could see the fur on a fold of her belly begin to pulsate as one of them, struggling upwards, partially emerged into the light before being pushed back into hiding. For long hours Ripple slept the contented sleep of motherhood, her head resting on her back or rudder, her eyes almost closed but still showing white through small slits.

If the lamp was left full on for too long the heat caused her discomfort, so I kept the rheostat on low and only turned it up when I thought some activity was imminent. Most of the time the cubs slept, their heads buried in Ripple's soft fur, while she encircled them with her body. Sometimes she turned round through 180 degrees, still concealing them. After a three-hour wait the cubs began to squeak softly and nuzzled at their mother's belly. She raised her head and turned round so that I could see both of them searching for her teats. They suckled vigorously and quite audibly, wagging their little tails from side to side and kneading Ripple's stomach with their front paws.

They fed for about ten minutes and when they had finished, Ripple turned each over on to its back in turn and steadying it between her front paws, licked the anal region. This stimulated the cub to relieve itself with much tail wagging, Ripple licking up the faeces as they were voided.

All three soon settled down to another spell of sleeping and there was no further activity during the next hour, after which I left them.

I spent many days watching and they seemed to suckle about once every three or four hours, though sometimes at somewhat shorter intervals. When the cubs were fourteen days old the male weighed $10\frac{1}{2}$ ounces and the female $9\frac{3}{4}$ ounces. At thirty days their eyes were still tightly closed and only opened fully after a further eight days which was later than the previous litter. By that time they were more mobile and crawled about the holt. Ripple continued to lick them after each bout of suckling and to eat their faeces until the cubs were just over seven weeks old. By then they had taken to following her outside the holt in the evening and a week later they were relieving themselves a few feet away from the entrance. At that time they were still suckling and made no attempt to eat solid food.

In the wild, the female otter brings fish or other food into the holt for the cubs and so I put live roach in Ripple's pool, hoping to film her returning with one. This she did on several occasions, but the cubs were just over nine weeks old before one of them began to nibble a fish. By that time they were

steadier on their feet and beginning to romp all over their enclosure at dusk.

My filming sessions continued and during the next fortnight
the youngsters grew more active and learned to eat solid food,
especially fresh fish, avidly, though I still saw them suckle
when they were eleven weeks old, by which time the male's
scrotum was quite noticeable as were the pale patches on their
necks and chests. Their evening games became more boisterous and when they were seventy-nine days old I saw the male
enter the pool for the first time, though both of them had often
played at the edge and put their heads in. Once again Ripple
made no effort to encourage her cubs to take to the water or to
teach them to swim.

Otters are born travellers, rarely staying long in one place,
and a bitch whose cubs are strong, active and able to swim is
likely to leave the breeding holt and move on with her family.
What contact, if any, the dog otter has with them is a matter of
conjecture, but from my own observations I think he often
accompanies them. During their travels the family may lie up
in the usual burrow type of holt or make 'couches' of flattened
vegetation in the middle of a reed bed, a particularly popular
place in Norfolk, or in thick cover near water. These couches
are rather similar to the 'platforms' made by coypu.

In order to continue the story of an otter's life I needed to
film the next stage and to do this I had to find a small manage-
able stream, a stretch of which could be wired in to form a
natural set without risk of losing the otters. After a good deal
of searching with the help of a farmer friend, we found the
ideal place and as he knew the landowner we were given per-
mission to put up the necessary fence so that we had an otter-
proof enclosure some fifty yards long. The stream, about three
paces wide, meandered lazily through low-lying meadows, its
clear water rippling over stretches of gravel or swirling silently
in deeper pools beneath the alders. Its banks were overgrown
with bramble, nettles and purple loosestrife while tussocks of
tufted sedge and clumps of meadowsweet invaded the damper
places. Further down, the water tumbled over a small weir and

cascaded into the broad shallows of the ford lying shrouded in the shade of oaks and chestnut. A narrow foot-bridge spanned the weir and standing on it the scene always reminds me of Constable's 'Haywain'.

It was too much to expect Ripple to make a couch for her cubs, but fortunately I had photographed several during my study of otters in the wild a year or two earlier, and now I made life-like replicas at the water's edge within the enclosure.

One sunny March day when the crocuses were already ablaze and the metallic notes of great tits rang from the hedgerows, when thrushes sang and skylarks climbed joyously towards the clouds, when spring had announced its arrival, we took Ripple and her cubs to the stream.

I set up the camera opposite one of the couches which we had carefully constructed in a natural hollow in the bank, partially screened by rushes and overhung with brambles. The two cubs were curled up happily in their warm nest and occasionally a small head would peer over the edge and gaze intently at the silvery water rippling beneath; soon they would be venturing for the first time into the wide world of a real stream.

Released from her travelling box, Ripple slipped into the water and immediately swam upstream to her cubs as if she knew exactly where we had put them. Reassured, she explored the whole enclosure, running round the perimeter netting before returning to the water where she dived and swam, disappearing beneath the overhanging bank only to reappear in the least expected places. I particularly wanted to film her taking a fish to the cubs, so Roy threw her a small roach, one of half a dozen supplied by a friendly angler. Ripple dived and took it with ease, furthermore she turned and swam towards the couch. It seemed too good to be true – the camera was running, following her movements through the waterside undergrowth until she reached the cubs. A moment's pause and she carried straight on, still with the fish in her mouth, until she reached the water's edge and there she ate it beneath an overhanging willow. She did exactly the same thing with the second and the third fish, but the fourth she dropped casually in the couch as she passed and both cubs quickly pounced on it, bickering as each tried to gain sole possession.

Later that day as the shadows lengthened and the sedge flies emerged for their one night of courtship before the water claimed their spent bodies, the cubs decided to explore the river bank. At first they ventured only a few feet and the slightest noise or movement sent them scurrying back to their nest; but gradually they went further afield and paddled at the very edge of the stream. Their coats soon became wet and they looked like a couple of drowned rats, for as yet their fur lacked the waterproof quality of an adult's coat. One cub, the male, whom we had christened Cockle, was bolder than Clam, his sister, and often explored on his own. Once he caught sight of Ripple devouring a fish beneath her favourite willow where a bend in the stream formed a tiny beach. He ran up to her and attempted to share the meal but Ripple turned on him, swearing and snapping at his face, until he retreated; a few moments later he tried again, only to receive the same hostile reception.

We spent several sunny spring days with the otter family on that stream and gradually the cubs grew up, their coats shed the water and they swam fearlessly, spending little time in the couches but exploring every inch of both banks, playing hide-and-seek round the trees and in the thickets of bramble and nettle. Ripple left them to themselves much of the time, though she always knew just where to find them. She delighted in a small deep pool which the river had carved out at the foot of the curving bank. A fallen tree shaded the water which swirled lazily through its trailing branches, forming a series of small eddies. It was in this pool that she caught numerous sticklebacks. Surfacing after a successful dive she crunched the fish while swimming. Had the quarry been larger, she would have taken it ashore before eating it.

Otters are constantly on the move within their territory, and this may include a five- or six-mile stretch of river. There are probably several reasons for this semi-nomadic existence. In the first place an otter needs a large territory in order to find sufficient food to survive, and constant wandering ensures that no part of its home range is overfished. Then there is the safety factor: an animal that is here one day and gone the next is less likely to run into trouble, and the otter is without doubt one of the most secretive and elusive of all our wild creatures.

It was necessary to show this constant wandering in the film and this meant having otters tame enough to go free even in the sea. We were fortunate in having Fury who still retained her early dog-like attachment to Barbara, while Kate and Lucy were totally imprinted on Jeanne and me though they were too young as yet to play the part of full-grown otters. During the summer, therefore, the brunt of the filming fell on Fury who responded with obvious enjoyment mounting to excitement once she realized what was in store when carried from the enclosure to the car.

She at once made it clear that she hated being put in a box of any kind, so we allowed her to travel loose in the car. This was fine for Barbara who was on the best of terms with her, but not so good for Roy, who usually drove, since Fury was decidedly unreliable with men. The first time they set off for the river all went well until Fury decided to lie across the back of Roy's seat with her head resting on his shoulder. Not content with that she suddenly thrust her bewhiskered nose into his left ear with the result that the car swerved across the road.

It soon became apparent that with Fury running free in the river and behaving just like a wild otter, we had a unique chance to observe in daylight all those facets of otter behaviour that normally occur only under cover of darkness.

When we reached the location Barbara carried Fury in her arms to the river's edge while we set up the camera. Released, Fury always made for the water to swim and drink since otters soon become dehydrated in warm weather, even on a half-hour car journey. Then she explored both banks in turn, looking for a suitable hiding place – a hole beneath the overhanging bank or amongst the roots of a waterside tree. Field drains and neighbouring ditches were also a source of particular interest, though she never wandered far at first and if she lost contact with us would utter that ultra high-pitched whistle or squeak which is the otter's contact note.

Although hand-reared from an early age, Fury had no difficulty in catching small fish and eels right from the start, and I was surprised at the apparent ease with which she accomplished it. The weir pool was her favourite place and she liked nothing better than to dive and roll in the white foam beneath the cascading water, bobbing up amidst the fast-flowing bubbles only to disappear again in search of eels lurking in the dim grey world beneath the weir sill.

Otters are easily bored – perhaps this is another reason for their nomadic life – and we soon found that Fury refused to stay long in one area. Having explored its possibilities, searched its hidden depths, investigated the labyrinth of overgrown banks, she moved on and if we were not to lose contact we had to follow. One day she had become intent on hunting a certain waterside bramble thicket when suddenly a duck mallard rocketed skywards, quacking in alarm as Fury pushed her muzzle into its down-filled nest. Eggs did not interest her so she moved on, only to send a brood of young moorhens skittering across the water from their hideout amongst the sedge. Fury dived in pursuit and presently surfaced, a small be-draggled body in her jaws. She brought it to the bank and lay in the shallows champing noisily; it was then that I discovered she had found not a baby moorhen but a drowned fledgeling blackbird which must have fallen to its death on its maiden flight from a nearby nest.

The lush meadows bordering the stream were grazed by a herd of Jersey cows. Every afternoon, soon after four o'clock, the herd returned from milking, straggled down the track from the farm and forded the shallows above the weir. Some stopped to drink, others, stimulated by the cold water, defecated, while others cropped the fresh wayside grass until urged forward by the cowman's noisy shouts. Fury showed no particular fear of cows though she kept her distance, but strange human voices sent her dashing into the nearest cover to lie low until danger passed. At first we thought we had lost her until we realized she might remain hidden for as long as she could hear any strange voices – and her hearing was far more sensitive than ours.

How does such a secretive solitary animal as the otter find its mate at the right moment? This was a question I had often pondered. One summer's afternoon we took Fury to the stream to continue filming. In mid-June the dank riverside jungle had reached maturity. A tangled mass of full-sapped growth overhung the water, dragonflies flickered in flashes of green and peacock blue across the stream, turtle doves crooned from the many trees and the air was sweet with the scent of fresh-mown hay.

Upon reaching the bank Fury immediately showed signs of great excitement. She ran downstream towards the weir, crossed the brook and busily hunted the bank, recrossing far below and turning back towards us. Just short of the weir she paused, sniffing intently at a patch of short grass beneath the alder tree not far from the foot-bridge. Suddenly stopping, with her rudder arched, she urinated, then ran a few yards before returning to the same spot to urinate again. She repeated this three times and for the rest of the afternoon her attention was torn between the lure of the river and the even stronger attraction of that patch of grass.

It was easy to tell that Fury was in oestrus both from her swollen vulva and the constant urinating; her fixation on that one patch of grass meant only one thing – a dog otter had passed that way during the night and had chosen this spot to leave his message. Fury had responded to his call and had she been a wild otter would no doubt have met her would-be spouse. As things were he may well have followed her trail eagerly a few nights later, only to give up perplexed at its sudden end.

An otter's coat is waterproof only if kept in immaculate condition and this means regular and frequent drying. Every half-hour or so Fury left the stream to rub herself dry, writhing snake-like from side to side, her belly prostrate and her chin furrowing the short grass. Fresh molehills were always her first choice, and the crumbly soil seemed to absorb surplus moisture quickly so that her coat soon became covered with earth which disappeared the moment she shook her fur sleek and dry.

Not all Fury's time was spent exploring the waterways or hunting for fish. Like all otters she was very playful and quick to discover new games: an eel caught, bitten and released only to be grabbed again and thrown into the air in a cat and mouse chase, a submerged attack on a floating feather, a piece of bark to be seized from below and clasped to her chest by her fore-paws as she floated on her back, carried along by the fickle current, all these and many more gave expression to her sense of fun.

Otters living near the sea often spend much of their time on the shore, particularly where estuaries and fresh marshes meet the tide and make it easy for them to move from one environment to the other. Sea lochs are another favourite haunt, especially those in Ireland and on the west coast of Scotland where there are long empty stretches of secluded coastline, ideal for otters. There they often move up the rivers and burns to hunt for trout in the freshwater lochs and sometimes the young are born far from the sea with only curlews and other moorland birds for company.

The great salt marshes of the north Norfolk coast with their maze of muddy creeks and the close proximity of fresh marsh and rivers support a few otters, though nothing like as many as the wilder and more remote northern shores. I was anxious to show this side of an otter's life, so we decided to film Fury out on the tide edge amongst the sea-lavender, spartina and wheeling gulls. It was high summer and from mid-morning onwards visitors could be expected sometimes right out at the edge of the more remote saltings. Furthermore people often took their dogs for a walk along the beach, and as strange dogs constituted perhaps the most serious menace to a tame otter, I decided that filming must finish before eleven o'clock which meant being on location at eight in the morning. Since the coast looks its best at full tide it was necessary to confine our activities to those periods of the month when the tide was high early in the morning and hope the day would be sunny.

We chose the Stiffkey marshes as being among the least disturbed and as soon as conditions seemed right Roy and Barbara set off with Fury in the Mini pick-up while we followed in a car laden with equipment. Half an hour later we bumped down the track below the disused army camp and drove along the hard ground at the edge of the marsh until we reached the wooden foot-bridge across the main creek. There we parked the vehicles and having divided the equipment between Roy, Jeanne and myself we started on the mile-long walk to the saltings' edge. Barbara carried Fury in her arms, for speed was essential and I knew that if she put the otter down in such strange surroundings our progress would be hopelessly slow. As we crossed the foot-bridge I noticed that the creek was already nearly full, the muddy water flecked with foam and marsh debris still hurrying landwards on the incoming tide.

The morning air was fresh and as we made our way through the sea-lavender, zig-zagging to and fro to avoid the wider creeks and jumping the smaller ones, redshanks flew up on all sides shrieking their alarm calls. Meadow pipits rose at our feet and overhead skylarks sang in the pale blue sky, while out at the tide's edge the terns streamed seaward to begin the day's fishing.

It says much for both Barbara and Fury that we reached without mishap the edge of the salting where the sea takes over in clumps of spartina and glistening mud. Setting up the camera we went on to meet the tide which was creeping steadily across the sandbars, filling the wind-blown runnels, moving on towards the land, the silken rustle of its progress broken only by the sound of the wind and the cries of sea-birds. Looking at the girl with the otter, both of them very small against the limitless seascape, I felt suddenly anxious. What would Fury make of it? Would she swim out to sea never to be heard of again? Would she perhaps disappear in the labyrinth of creeks and gullies behind us?

To seaward in the north-east I could make out the Binks, a

raised sandbar upon which the sandwich terns were nesting. The combination of distance, sunlight and water made it shimmer as the rising tide licked its slopes, while far beyond, the fir trees of Wells Marsh appeared to rise out of the sea. As Barbara put Fury down at the water's edge the terns rose in a screaming horde to mob a passing skua.

Far from running away or swimming out to sea Fury showed signs of agoraphobia in her new dimension and at first kept very close to Barbara – so close that it was difficult to film her. Gradually her confidence returned and she began to explore the shallow inroads made by the advancing tide. Soon she was swimming and diving freely in the deeper water of the small creeks and pushing her way through clumps of sea-lavender and rice-grass growing on the muddy ridges. Suddenly she seemed to sense the sea and emerging from a gully ran off across the open sand towards the tide-edge, flushing a pair of ringed plovers on the way.

The line of waves, scarcely more than large ripples, deterred her and she went on along the beach to investigate a mussel scaup which being on a slight bank was not yet covered. A pair of oystercatchers, whose newly-hatched chicks crouched like small pebbles on the shingle ridge behind us, were busily probing amongst the stones and mussels, turning over the dark flat fronds of seaweed with their long bills.

At the sight of the otter they rose screaming, then dived in mock attack, their black and white plumage etched against the blue sea, their carmine bills flashing angry alarm calls. Fury seemed quite unperturbed so that first one bird and then the other landed protesting a few yards away and tried to lure her further from their nesting territory by running along just in front. Their ruse worked and soon Fury found herself back at the water's edge. This time she was braver and after retreating before two or three wavelets she took the plunge and was soon enjoying yet another new sensation – and what fun she had ducking through the waves and diving for the first time in the open sea! Finding herself all alone, she turned and swam parallel with the shore, heading our way. When she was on the surface we could see the thin black line of her wash drawn on the mirror-flat water, but otters are not really designed to swim on the surface for long, and her progress consisted of a series of dives, coming up between each to take several breaths and get her bearings.

As in the river, Fury soon lost interest in one stretch of shore and was constantly on the move, so that we had to follow in order to film all her adventures. Instinctively she worked her way back towards the land, recrossing the shingle-ridge at the edge of the salting and pausing to explore the clumps of white sea-campion, heavy with belled flowers up-turned towards the sun, and yellow-horned poppy growing in profusion amongst the stones. This brought her very close to the downy young of the oystercatchers who redoubled their mobbing with hysterical shrieks.

The strand line at the edge of the marsh where previous high tides had left a trail of wrack and rubbish yielded up all sorts of sea-borne treasures – a small child's beach shoe, the sun-shrivelled cases of skates' eggs, the grape-like clusters of dried up whelks' eggs and innumerable plastic containers. One of these, bearing the name of a well-known household detergent, amused Fury who found that, helped by the breeze, she could easily dribble it along the beach with her nose.

Some way to the west a large creek left the shelter of the salt-marsh and carved its way seawards through the sandbars. At low tide it held only a trickle of water, its steep banks of glistening mud topped by an overhanging fringe of sea-lavender. The great salting was veined with minor creeks and gullies, many of which fed this one. Now at the top of the tide, with twelve feet of water and a maze of hidden retreats, it was an otter's paradise and Fury's favourite place.

The sand at the mouth of the creek was yellow and firm and there we set up the camera, moving from time to time to comply with Fury's whims. Sometimes she disappeared in the wilderness of sea-lavender only to reappear several minutes later when we were beginning to be anxious. The creek proved a rich fishing ground, and she often surfaced with a small flounder clamped in her jaws. Swimming to the edge, she hauled out and champed it up. Small crabs, called 'gillys' in Norfolk, caused her endless amusement and I was lucky enough to film her surfacing with an unusually large one which was very much alive. Holding it in her mouth she was plainly bewildered by the mass of struggling, prickly legs and even more disconcerted when one of its pincers clamped on to her upper lip. Seizing the crab in her front paws she shook her head violently, whipping the water to foam. The crab transferred its grip to a paw which resulted in even more violent shaking. Dislodged, it sidled off down into the muddy depths, but Fury, not to be beaten, dived in pursuit and soon reappeared on the surface where the scene was re-enacted. This happened three times and in the end, I'm glad to say, the crab won.

While we were filming I became conscious of a rowing boat approaching behind me and when I looked round a man was standing in the water a few yards away. Apparently he had been there for some time but so gentle were his movements and so much part of the seascape his demeanour that neither Fury nor I had noticed him. He was warden of the marsh and had come to see what was going on. I was delighted to learn from him that at dusk only a few nights before he had watched a wild otter fishing in this very creek.

Another favourite haunt of Fury's was a wide creek further to the east called the Freshers which, fed in its tortuous crawl across the wide saltings by a tangle of lesser creeks, channels and runnels, formed the mouth of the Stiffkey River. Further inland it looped through the village, its banks crowded with cottage gardens, its slow waters lazily reflecting the greys and blues of old houses and farm premises built of traditional Norfolk flints.

Beyond the farm the river coiled across the lush water meadows beneath rolling uplands rich in woods that teemed with pheasants. This was the valley where Henry Williamson once farmed. Bullocks still stand knee-deep in the ford in the heat of summer, fat trout lie in clear pools and swallows dart under the old iron bridge which carries the twisting coast road. To seaward are more thistle-strewn meadows and then the river makes its final bow via a great steel sluice in the green sea-wall. From that point its identity is lost in a tidal world of sea-lavender, asters, gold-dusted purslane and gleaming mud.

I well remember one early July morning when we reached the coast soon after dawn while the sun was struggling to break through a film of low-lying cloud. Cattle moved across the fresh marsh like ships, their legs hidden in a fog of white mist. The morning air was still and cool, laden with sea scents and as we drove through the gorse and along the track to our parking place at the edge of the salting we saw that the tide was exceptionally high, for the whole marsh lay beneath a glimmering sheet of water broken here and there by low banks of seablite and tussocks of cord grass.

To obtain an otter's eye view we wanted to get some really low-angle shots of Fury which meant lying in the water with a hand-held camera so that the lens was only two or three inches above the surface. After I had put on the bottom half of my wet suit we set off, Barbara carrying Fury in her arms and Roy helping with the equipment. Already the water was beginning to move almost imperceptibly towards the shore, for in these parts the sea only visits the saltings twice for two brief hours in every twenty-four.

After fording several brimming gullies we reached a wide creek too deep to cross, so we put Fury down amongst the sea-lavender and, lying on my stomach, I filmed her as she furrowed her way through the purple spikes. Sometimes the water was just deep enough for her to slide beneath the surface, a string of bubbles and moving stalks marking her course. As the water dropped she found a maze of secret caverns carved by successive tides in the firm mud, hidden beneath the fringe of vegetation at the edge of every gully. Soon the water gathered momentum and whispered seawards, the bare mud hissing as the air filled its drying pores.

We caught occasional glimpses of Fury when she climbed

out of one gully and loped a few yards across the marsh before disappearing into the next. Once she vanished without trace for twenty minutes and we began to worry, then we saw her right back at the edge of the salting, exploring the gorse and bramble thickets.

Calling her name, Barbara trudged back, but Fury was enjoying herself flushing rabbits and fledgeling birds and it was a full half-hour before she came out and we set off once more for the tide edge.

Beyond the marsh the sea had already retreated towards the main Stiffkey channel leaving bars of golden sand, clinging mud and dark mussel scaups.

The young 'seed' mussels are carefully tended by the long-shoremen, who plant, guard and on the cold winter days when the ice pans crunch in the creeks, harvest the full-grown molluscs. They bring their haul home in flat-bottomed boats and then, in the lee of the boat house, their fingers stiff and blue with the cold, they riddle and grade the mussels.

At this season a film of ice follows the retreating tide across the mud flats, where flocks of small, dark-bellied brent geese, their white sterns flashing, paddle the plashes, their musical 'cronks' carrying far on the wind.

Fury discovered the mussel beds with joy, for here were innumerable small pools, crystal clear and full of darting shore-shrimps easy to catch and crunch. Fishing in the main tideway was even more productive and soon she was diving for flukes and enjoying her catch on the nearest sandbar.

Out on the tide-line curlews, newly returned from nesting places on inland heaths, called plaintively. Redshanks, ringed plovers and oystercatchers flew up and down the shore, while overhead common and little terns looking like large white swallows flew to and fro between their hungry nestlings on Blakeney Point and their fishing grounds in the channel and beyond. Two or three sometimes left the main procession to mob Fury, diving over her head with harsh screams, but the otter took little notice as she busied herself exploring plashes and pools.

While Fury enjoyed many such mornings on the coast, Kate and Lucy were being encouraged to swim. At first we had filmed them playing on the banks of a nearby brook. They were then three months old and their rough and tumble wrestling matches often took them to the water's edge; they did a little hesitant paddling, but went no further. Pieces of bark, the sun-dried hollow stalks of old thistles, feathers and a half shell of a moorhen's egg were all discovered and played with briefly, for nothing occupied them for long.

When they were four months old we decided they ought to begin swimming lessons, not that they needed to be taught, but they had at first a certain fear of water and needed to gain confidence. We took them to the Tearoom pool in the Park every evening and, wearing wellingtons, paddled in the shallows calling to the cubs to follow. To begin with they ran up and down at the water's edge squeaking, not wanting to be left behind but not daring to take the plunge. Lucy, always more fearless than Kate, soon waded out to the limit of her depth, then keeping her hind feet firmly on the bottom she paddled with her front paws until one evening she found she could swim just as Fury had done before her. From then on we encouraged them by throwing twigs and sticks just ahead of them. Both cubs learnt to retrieve them and it was not long before Lucy and Kate were swimming happily around the pool.

We spent many summer afternoons with them in various locations along the upper reaches of the River Stiffkey where we had previously filmed Fury. The water meadows were dry and firm enough for us to drive the car along the bank which saved lugging the heavy equipment and also meant that the cubs had a focal point to which to return. A wandering cow, or the gamekeeper's voice was enough to send them both scampering up the bank to dive to safety beneath the vehicle.

On their first excursion both spent most of the time exploring the banks deep with the growth of summer, playing hide-and-seek in thickets of meadowsweet, dodging between the waving stems of purple valerian and clumps of meadow rue. But the water's edge attracted them most and their favourite pastime was sludging in the black mud amongst beds of wild watercress, crowsfoot and kingcups. Sedge warblers rasped their monotonous song from the tangle of reed and bramble; a whitethroat, whose flimsy nest of dried grasses was hidden in a sea of nettles and briars, scolded the cubs with harsh churring notes. For Lucy and Kate it was an exciting world.

Lucy soon swam across the stream to explore the opposite bank, leaving Kate squeaking hysterically in the shallows. Finding she was alone Lucy turned back, ran up to her sister and pushing her nose against Kate's two or three times (an otter's form of affectionate greeting), encouraged her to follow. Kate set off, but once in the water her nerve failed her. Again Lucy turned back to her sister, who, reassured, followed her across the brook. I was lucky enough to capture the whole episode on film.

Once over their initial fear, their swimming improved rapidly and they began to range further up and down the river. Dark holes, caves and caverns, field drains and overgrown ditches intrigued them while the deep recesses carved by winter spates beneath the roots of waterside trees always lured them in.

A few furlongs below the weir on the west bank stands an ash tree, knee-deep in water. Two enormous roots jut out like grey fangs into the river bed and between them lies a dark hollow in which the water laps and gurgles. This was a favourite hideout for the cubs, for the stream outside is deep enough for a submerged entry, while immediately opposite on the far bank a rotting willow stump offers two smaller retreats overhung with bramble. Quite often we lost contact, sometimes for twenty minutes or more – but while we became anxious, the cubs were quite happy so long as they could hear us calling their names. Doubtless they considered these noises our normal contact notes. Whenever they vanished we were careful to inspect the hollow beneath the ash tree. Lying on my stomach, the cold stream licking my chin, I could peer inside at water level and sometimes I was rewarded by the dim outline of a flat bewhiskered nose and two tiny eyes.

When it was time to go home the cubs discovered they could play us up for ages by diving and swimming to and fro between the ash tree and the willow stump. Then we pretended to leave them, often driving the car a few hundred yards in an attempt to convince them we were going. This ruse worked sometimes, but not always.

During these filming excursions Kate and Lucy demonstrated just how sensitive an otter is to the most subtle tones of sound. While we called them in a normal voice they remained confident and usually made some movement which betrayed their whereabouts. But if we had lost them and became anxious, especially if danger in the form of a strange dog threatened, our tone clearly relayed our fears to the cubs whose reaction was to freeze wherever they were and remain hidden until the danger had passed, which they judged had happened only when our voices relaxed. Once we realized this we tried our hardest to sound perfectly normal whatever our fears, but it was no use, they detected the merest trace of anxiety as if by telepathy.

Lucy had been swimming only three weeks when she caught her first fish and, lying beside her in the shallows, I saw her do it. Below the ash tree with hollowed roots the stream widened and runs each side of a shingle spit. Under the far bank the water tumbled over stones and sand, the sunlight flickering brightly on its rippled surface. Deeper water lay beneath the near bank where the movement slowed, and eddies of winter floods had scoured small holes in the stream bed. The deepest part just topped a man's knee and a fringe of green weed waved lazily in the current the length of the shingle spit. I had often noticed shoals of small fish lying in these holes, always ready to dart into the protecting weed at the slightest movement.

While Kate was busy sludging through the dank ooze in the twilight world of the overhanging bank, Lucy swam out into the sunlight, dipped her head and slid beneath the surface to explore the hollow. The small fish flashed like silver sparks as they disappeared into the thick weed. Lucy, only three feet from my face and in crystal clear water, turned and nosed through the waving fronds like a spaniel quartering a beet field. A short stabbing lunge, and she rolled over, bobbing up with a stickleback in her mouth. Thrilled by her first success she lay on her back, borne by the current, juggling the fish in her front paws.

Though Kate was greedier than Lucy, she took longer to discover that live food lurked beneath the stones on the river bed and skulked in the thickets of waving weed, but once she found out she too became a highly competent fisherman. Both cubs had convinced me that fishing is an inherited part of the otter's life pattern. But how did they find fish in the muddy waters of tidal creeks, by what means did they detect slippery eels in the dark recesses of the mill leat? Exactly what happened down in the dark, mysterious depths of the otters' secret world? There was only one way to find out and that was to follow them and share their underwater adventures. This I resolved to do.

7. World beneath the Water

Sitting on the bottom in the deep end of Norwich Public
Baths in fifteen feet of water, I became aware that Mallory, my
diving instructor, was signalling to me to remove my mouthpiece and pass it to him. This was part of the training, so taking
a couple of deep breaths I handed over my life-giving air
supply. I remember that Mallory seemed to be ages taking his
two breaths before passing it back to me.

Looking up through the bottle-green chlorinated water I
saw boys swimming on the surface like distant pink frogs. Later
I was taught to swim up from the bottom holding hands with
Mallory and sharing one mouthpiece. This is a safety measure
which ensures survival should one diver of a pair suffer a
sudden failure in his air supply when deep down.

This course of instruction in skin diving took place some
years earlier when I was trying to shoot some underwater film
of seals for Anglia Television. The seal pool in the Park is one
of the largest in Europe and in it I kept six common and one
pair of big Atlantic grey seals. Nobody knew what the seals
would do when encountering a skin diver in their pool for the
first time and I was particularly apprehensive about the bull
grey seal who tended to be aggressive and had a savage bite.

One July evening we decided the time had come to find out
their reaction. Putting on my wet suit and equipment, I slid
below the surface, leaving Mallory similarly equipped and
ready to come to my rescue if anything went wrong. A few late
visitors to the Park leant on the surrounding rail and watched
our antics with interest. My first shock was to discover that
while the pool had been scrubbed out and refilled with pure
water from a deep bore which looked clear from the surface,
visibility below was only four feet at the most. I found myself
swimming along in a grey mist in which hung particles of fish
upon which the seals had been feeding. I made two complete

circuits of the pool without seeing so much as the tip of a seal's flipper. Surfacing, I took off my face mask to find the on-lookers highly amused, for no sooner had I dived than all the seals had left the water in consternation and flapped out on to the safety of the rocky island in the middle from which they kept peering down into the pool! I can only think that they had mistaken the noise of my aqualung for a killer whale or some other predator.

It took us three weeks of nightly practice before the seals accepted us and even then they tended to give us a fairly wide berth with the exception of a young female common seal called Gamma. Curiosity seemed to get the better of her, and she often swam right up to me and peered into my face mask. I teased her by tweaking her tail flipper as she turned to swim away.

Seals may be clumsy on land but in their natural element they are masters of grace. Able to swim just as fast and effort-lessly on their backs as on their fronts, they sped past me like grey torpedoes, driven forward by the powerful sculling strokes of their hind flippers. Such was their speed that we found it difficult to hold them in view for long enough to film them.

In the end we discovered the only way was for Mallory to swim along on the surface, wearing goggles and carrying some sprats in a bucket. Looking down he could see me kneeling on the bottom of the pool and whenever a seal approached he dropped a sprat a few feet in front of the camera.

Now I was determined to follow the otters wherever they dived in river, lake or sea, but I knew we should have difficulty with poor visibility when trying to film them. There would be a further problem when they chased fish in open waters for I should not be able to keep up with them however fast I flippered and they would be unlikely to catch their quarry within a few feet of my camera unless I was extraordinarily lucky.

To overcome these problems we decided that for some of the underwater shots we would build a film set of natural rock, stones and old tree stumps in the beaver pool in the Park. This pool is thirty feet long and almost as wide with a depth of six feet. The beavers were removed to temporary quarters and we set about reconstructing the bed of a stream. The result looked rather disappointing when seen from the bank, but remarkably life-like from below the surface, especially with the addition of reeds and water weed anchored in the pebble-strewn floor.

Once again we had trouble with visibility despite thorough scrubbing of the concrete pool and washing every weed and stone before use, for even without an otter in the pen the water became murky within hours. The BBC consulted experts who analysed the water. The cause, they said, was the growth of algae and the cure a diatomaceous earth filtration plant which operated by a powerful electric pump would filter the entire volume of the pool every six hours. The plant was installed and worked wonders, producing what is known technically as polished water. It ran day and night and even with Fury living in the enclosure visibility remained perfect.

Unlike the seals Fury showed no fear of the strange under-water snoring and bubbling of my aqualung and I shall never forget the first afternoon I spent in the pool. The water gushing from the outlet pipe of the filtration plant created a lazy current, and made the sunlight dance in concentric waves on the pebble bottom. The clumps of weed bobbed and swayed and a shoal of roach hung suspended head to current in the shade cast by a large willow stump, their gills moving rhyth-mically, their silver-scaled sides flashing in the sunlight whenever they moved out of the shadow.

Viewed from above, a shoal of fish appear to lie one behind the other as a skein of geese or gulls appear to fly when seen from the ground. In their own element it immediately becomes apparent that individuals, while conforming to the pattern, adjust their depth or altitude so as to avoid their neighbour's wash or slipstream.

It is a surprising fact that most writers when describing the underwater movement of otters have been wide of the mark. Far from paddling with all four feet to increase speed, Fury demonstrated that the otter's main propulsion stems from powerful vertical strokes of the entire lumbar region with additional kicks every now and then from the hind feet, the front feet being held close to the body to complete the stream-lining.

Upon diving an otter emits the string of bubbles so familiar to anyone who has observed these animals. Watching Fury I noticed that the bubbles came from the corners of her mouth, curled upwards and united, rising as a single stream from her nape. A second string, in line with the first, emanated from her back at the base of her rudder. This was caused by air trapped between the outer guard hairs and the inner dense fur of her coat being forced back along her body by the pressure of the water.

Fury used her front paws with webbed toes spread wide for maximum effect, as well as her rudder, when turning at speed, but she paddled only with all four feet when cruising slowly on the surface, usually with her head above water but sometimes ducking to peer down into the depths beneath. I had always wondered just how otters caught fish and whether they had to work hard for their living. Now, lying at ease on the bottom of the pool I was able to observe and film the pursuit and capture of quarry not once but many times and subsequently to see the same action in the wild in both fresh and salt water.

Fury spent much of her time playing beneath the surface, exploring the granite rocks and diving under the roots and trunk of a dead willow that we had anchored securely on the bottom in the deepest place. Often she swam through the shoal of roach which parted like curtains while she passed, drawing together again as soon as she had gone.

When she was hungry and chasing the fish in earnest their reaction was quite different. The shoal scattered at her ap-proach soon to re-form, while the chosen victim fled before the otter. Fury was always master of the situation and had no difficulty in following the fish. Sometimes she took one in her front paws, usually attacking from beneath, for fish cannot see directly downwards. If in a playful mood and not hungry she often released the victim unharmed, but when meaning to kill she seized even quite a large fish in her front paws, biting it and surfacing with the quarry in her mouth. Eels, and sometimes other fish, were usually pursued and caught by a slashing sideways bite, often to be dropped and snatched again. The resistance of the eel is its misfortune, for the twisting and thrashing of the writhing coils in a cloud of silver bubbles invariably stimulates an otter to play a cat and mouse game.

While not particularly afraid of snakes and indifferent to spiders, I have a horror of eels. An eel chased by an otter will seek refuge in the nearest cover and in my worst nightmare I saw a huge eel pursued by an even larger otter coming straight at me through a forest of slimy weed deep down in a mill pool, intent on wriggling to safety inside my wet suit via the collar opening.

It is said that the things you fear most don't happen and standing on the bridge by Bintree Mill gazing down into the depths of the pool fifteen feet below I fervently hoped it was true.

We had brought Fury to the mill to film her underwater and the owner, who took a keen interest in wildlife, had just told me that twenty-five tons of eels passed through the pool on their one and only migration to the sea during the months of July, August and September. Twenty-five tons and it was August and I was about to join them!

Inside the old wooden mill the air was cool and heavy with the dust of barley, stored in piled-up sacks. Everything was covered with a layer of grey flour which made us sneeze. Beneath the floorboards the pent-up river roared through the open sluices for the great mill wheel was still, and in its place an electric motor drove the grinding stones. As we turned the heavy crank handle the ratchet clattered on the cog and slowly the noise of the river died to a trickle.

Outside the sun shone, swallows skimmed the water feasting on the dancing clouds of flies, ringdoves cooed in the riverside willows and a paddling of domestic ducks were busy in the quiet reach above the old red brick bridge.

A hundred yards upstream beyond the mill the overflow

from the river swirled through another sluice, dived beneath a smaller bridge, eddied in a lesser pool and flowed through quiet meadows to the junction between leat and mainstream in the shade of a small coppice a furlong down river. The lawns of the owner's garden sloped down to the water on the opposite bank and downstream a fallen alder spanned the river.

While Fury explored this new territory I put on wet suit, air bottles and flippers before flapping awkwardly down the bank and into the shallows at the tail of the pool. The pungent smell of the river mingled with the scent of luxuriant waterside vegetation where willow herb, purple loosestrife and ragged robin grew among a tangle of nettles and sedge.

Moss and algae covered the dark stones beneath my feet, and as I waded deeper, trailing fronds of broad-leaved pondweed pulled at my legs. With the water up to my chest I stopped to look round. The mill was brilliant in the afternoon sun which threw dark shadows on the worn brickwork of the bridge and from near water level I could see into the gloomy cavern beneath, hear the trickle and splash of water in the dark distance and look up at the moss-covered brick arches which spanned the river in the dark culvert. I was beginning to see life from an otter's angle. Calling to Fury who was busy sludging at the waterside below the garden, I put on my face mask, adjusted the mouthpiece and plunged beneath the surface into a silence broken only by the rasp and bubble of my aqualung.

It was much darker than I had expected and the water uncomfortably cloudy so that swimming upstream I banged into boulders and struggled in dense mats of pondweed growing in the slacker water each side of the sluice. The grey shapes of fish, roach, dace and trout loomed before my eyes and faded into the foggy distance. They were unafraid, and as I swam slowly through the swaying forest of weed, I kept the camera running, often with shoals of small fish an arm's length away.

Dimly the moss-covered stonework of the sill appeared and looking up I could see the pale band of bubbles caught in the sunlight where the diminished stream cascaded beneath the sluice. Fury, slipping up from behind, dipped her head to peer into my camera lens and swam away in effortless undulations to vanish through the weed.

Moving slowly along the bottom I found a barren stretch at the foot of the stonework where the main river, released by the sluices, rushed on its way to the sea, for nothing but moss and algae could find a foothold and grow in such foaming turbulence now held back by the dropped gates.

If eels lurked, as I was certain they did, securely anchored by their muscular tails in current-carved crevices in the bricks and stone, I saw none, though shoals of fish flashed in psychedelic movement near the bright ceiling of the pool.

I found visibility improved considerably when I lay in five feet of water where the bottom shelved upwards towards the first shallows. Here more light penetrated and fewer bubbles obscured the view so that I could watch the world of the river in comparative comfort.

A waterlogged branch blown down by a winter gale and released from its muddy grave by a kick from one of my flippers rose slowly to the surface and drifted over my head, its sprawling arms trailing tresses of pondweed. Looking towards the deeper water below the sill I suddenly saw Fury shooting up towards the light, a large eel, at least two feet in length, writhing in her jaws. The current swept her into the middle of the pool and from my prone position I watched her play with her quarry. At the water's ceiling they rolled and twisted together, a tangle of webbed feet, tapered rudder and thrashing silver caught in an explosion of sun-drenched bubbles. Whenever Fury rose for air, scattering shafts of light, I could see only the submerged part of her body so that sometimes otter and eel became headless, since to a human diver looking up the surface appears as opaque as frosted glass. Once she let the eel go and it zig-zagged downwards away from the light only to be caught again and dragged along, trailing from Fury's jaws. Finally she disappeared as she swam with it into the shallows. Coming up I removed my mask and watched her as she lay in a few inches of water beneath the bank, the eel clasped firmly in her front paws, her head tilted as she chewed it.

Judging from its length the eel was a female, wearing its nuptial livery of bright silver belly and almost black back for the final journey of its life, the long swim to the unknown darkness in the depths of the Sargasso Sea, there to spawn and die. It had probably left that same sea twelve to twenty years ago as a tiny translucent flattish eel larva no more than 15 millimetres long to be borne northwards and eastwards by ocean currents for two and a half years before reaching our shores.

Already changed into a tiny eel or elver it had ascended this same stretch of river one spring day in search of some distant pond or lake, perhaps where its mother had grown and fattened before her sexual urge had driven her down to the distant sea.

This eel had fallen victim to Fury, but thousands like it were journeying down the river, changed from the bronze and yellow of adolescence into the silver and black of maturity. Already well into their final fast, for they would never feed again, their stomachs had begun to regress so that by the time the eels reached their birthplace the following spring their stomachs would have degenerated completely.

Crayfish like small grey-brown lobsters were not uncommon in the shallower and faster stretches of the river where it raced over ridges of gravel forming cascades of bubbles full of the oxygen these crustaceans need. Rarely more than three inches in length including their pincer claws, they were creatures of the dark, spending the day hiding under stones or in burrows in the banks. At night they came out to search for water-snails, tadpoles and other tiny creatures upon which they fed.

Fury was not long in discovering these tasty morsels and I saw her devour her first crayfish. She found it by accident while turning over small pebbles on the river's bed with her muzzle in search of a round stone to play with. This was a favourite game – having found one to her liking she would nose it along the bottom, surfacing with it in her front paws, juggling and sometimes balancing it on her chest or on her head.

Crayfish were even more fun to play with and several times I saw her nose one out and swim up to the top toying with it and allowing it to escape repeatedly in order to have the fun of re-capture. Finding itself free the crayfish flipped backwards, jerking its fan-shaped tail, heading at speed for the safety of the stones but was easily overtaken by the otter who, tiring of the sport, eventually ate it while swimming on the surface, dog-paddling slowly with her four webs, her body silhouetted against the sparkling ceiling of the pool.

As soon as Lucy and Kate were proficient swimmers we took them down to the river to study and film their underwater behaviour. At first they preferred the shallows so I was able to follow them wearing only the bottom half of my wet suit for warmth and using goggles and a snorkel rather than an air bottle.

Both cubs frequently caught sticklebacks by hunting for them in the dense jungles of hornwort and pondweed just as I had watched Lucy catch her first wild quarry several weeks earlier. The small gaily-coloured fish abound in the brackish creeks and dykes of the North Norfolk fresh marshes where they form an important part of the diet of wild otters.

Like Fury, the cubs loved to play underwater with round stones and since neither showed any fear of me they would often take them from my hand.

Kate was always much more highly-strung than Lucy and sometimes it was difficult to persuade her to leave the security of the car and follow her sister to the river only a few yards away. One afternoon in late summer we filmed them both play-ing together underwater in the clear reach below Bintree Mill where the leat rejoins the mainstream. Willows and alders line both banks and a swaying foot-bridge, one plank wide, spans the mouth of the leat where the current runs slow and deep.

Visibility underwater was fair at close range and I managed to persuade the cubs to play tug-of-war with a submerged branch in front of my camera. Jeanne waded nearby to give them confidence and on the bank an old man who had been mowing the waterside nettles, leant on his scythe and watched, silent and still as a grey heron. All went well until, moved to continue his labours, the man stoned his scythe. The sudden metallic noise was too much for Kate who rushed up the opposite bank and disappeared in the direction of the mill.

Hoping she was making for the car we followed, but of Kate there was no sign. Lucy had come with us when suddenly she stopped, then ran off and disappeared in a dense thicket of reed growing at the edge of the mill pool hard against the road bridge. Following her I caught a glimpse of both cubs playing happily in the seclusion of the swaying stalks.

There was nothing for it but to wait patiently until they felt like coming out. We sat down on the grass and before long, their curiosity getting the better of them, they crept out and approached our feet, only to dart back into cover the moment we moved. After an hour Lucy got bored and allowed Jeanne to pick her up and carry her to the car, but since it was far too hot to leave her there we decided that Jeanne should take her home while I sat by the reed bed and waited for Kate.

Half an hour after the car had left, the sun sank below the trees and a chill shadow crept across the grass. I wished I was wearing more than a pair of bathing trunks. I hadn't seen Kate for some time when suddenly she emerged. I spoke to her, but sat very still. She came closer, paused to sniff my toes then very slowly advanced. Waiting until she was well within reach I pounced with my left hand and seized her across the middle of the back. She rolled over on the grass and I tickled her stomach, then gathering her in my arms I walked away from the reed bed and sat with her in the most open place I could find, hoping that I should be able to hold her attention until Jeanne returned.

Kate seemed happy to be back with me and lolled in my lap yawning and clasping my wrist between her short front legs as I stroked her soft warm fur. The return journey would take Jeanne about forty-five minutes to which had to be added time to get Lucy out of the car and back into her enclosure via two doors, never an easy operation single-handed, especially if the otter was unco-operative and decided to skulk beneath the front seats which sometimes happened.

I felt sure Kate would stay with me provided no tractor or lorry with hissing air-brakes passed along the nearby road, and no low-flying aircraft came over us. Then she would be gone, for a frightened otter's immediate reaction is to bite very hard if restrained in any way. It was getting decidedly chilly and I was soon thankful for the warmth of Kate's body in my lap. Rather sooner than I dared hope I heard the car returning and we were quickly on the way home with Kate lying full-length along the shelf above the back seat looking out of the rear window.

As they grew, the cubs became more difficult to manage when taken out together, for they drew confidence from each other and sometimes went off exploring and then no amount of calling would induce them to return. Of course the more we called the more independent they became since they knew exactly where we were and had no fear of losing us though often we had no idea where they had gone.

North of the Park the land slopes down to the valley of the River Blackwater, a small, clear brook which joins the Wensum a couple of miles downstream. On its way it meanders through grazing meadows where in summer bullocks stand hock-deep in the cool water, swishing their tails in each other's faces to drive away the gadflies. There are poplars and willows and deep side dykes full of black ooze, overgrown and heavy with the cat-like scent of fleabane ignored by grazing beasts. In May nightingales sing in the dank coppices and build their leaf-lined nests beneath the sea of stinging nettles. On warm evenings snipe dive from the sky, stiff tail feathers producing their drumming notes of courtship.

Thanks to a friendly neighbour we spent many afternoons watching and filming Lucy and Kate in the stream, for not only was it close to home but we could drive the car some distance along one bank.

Usually we let both cubs out and when filming underwater
this doubled the chance of success. My method was to lie in
one of the deeper runs where there was just enough water to
cover both the camera and me while Jeanne slowly worked
the otters upstream in my direction. This was necessary because they often kicked up clouds of silt which discoloured the
water and reduced visibility downstream.

One day Kate decided to be particularly difficult: while
Lucy obediently sludged about near Jeanne, she kept swimming rapidly past my position to hunt the weed beds above,
sending down a constant stream of silt-laden water which made
filming impossible, so impossible that we had to give up. There
was nothing for it but to take Kate back to the car which we
had parked in the shade of a large alder.

Sensing that something was afoot she decided not to leave
the river and it took Jeanne half an hour of gentle persuasion
before she was able to grab Kate in the water as she swam by.
Carrying her to the car she shut her safely inside leaving all the
windows slightly open. Hitherto neither otter had ever ob-
jected to being left in the car, in fact they both seemed to
enjoy it and to feel secure there. We returned to the river and
went on filming Lucy.

Occasionally we heard Kate's high-pitched contact whistle,
but we took no notice until Lucy eventually heard it too and
ran back to the car. We followed and had difficulty in persuading her to come out from underneath. After a further
spell in the river she again ran back and this time refused to
leave the car. Inside Kate was chittering with rage and Lucy
kept standing up on her hind legs trying to find a way to
rescue her sister. It was only then that we looked through the
windows.

For some reason Kate, furious at being shut in, had spent her
time stripping the interior of the car with her teeth. Fortunately
she had ignored the leather seats and had concentrated on the
soft furnishing, ripping the carpet to shreds and tearing the
padded panels from the doors and door pillars. Neither of us
had ever seen the interior of a car so thoroughly wrecked and I

could imagine the reaction at the garage when I said it was all caused by a tame otter!

In their second summer Lucy and Kate spent still more time swimming with me while I filmed and photographed their activities underwater in the beaver pool as well as in local streams and in the sea. Of the two Lucy was easier to work, being less nervous of strange sights and sounds, though her independent nature was a drawback for she roamed far and wide and sometimes went missing for an hour or more. Nor was she always easy to pick up at the end of the day unless she happened to be in the mood.

Once we almost gave her up for lost. I had been swimming with her in the Blackwater River, taking shots of her playing with an eel she had caught in the mud beneath a mat of rushes and water crowfoot, when she dived and disappeared. Jeanne, who was keeping watch on the bank, had not seen her and we had no idea whether to look upstream or down. As the minutes passed with no sign of movement we discussed what to do. Jeanne felt she should stay where we had last seen her in case she returned and I set off upstream calling her name every few yards and scanning the water for a tell-tale ripple. The meadows were rank with the smell of fleabane and thistles scratched my bare legs, so whenever possible I waded in the river. Crouching in the dark shade of the brick archway carrying the road bridge, I searched for spraint on the concrete sill and found some, dark and sticky, but at least a week old. I thought Lucy might have used the wild otters' sprainting place had she passed that way.

Beyond the bridge two parallel fences of barbed wire barred the way with beds of tall nettles on either bank. Making a detour I went on upstream, catching fleeting glimpses of fish shadows darting ahead like dark arrows. Startled moorhens skittered along the surface before taking wing and once a pair of mallard jumped, the water from their paddles falling like drops of quicksilver caught in the sunlight.

Farther on the river divided and I wondered which course to follow, choosing the deeper which looked more promising. I walked and waded for another half-hour then gave up in despair and made my way back, still stopping to call every few yards, though with little conviction. All the time I felt sure Jeanne would have found her and the two of them would be waiting for me, but when I got back she had seen nothing though she too had kept calling at intervals.

I set off again, downstream this time, and noticed the long shadow walking ahead of me for the sun was low. A herd of bullocks, great South Devons, red as wine, stood in the shallows flicking their tails and tossing their heads at the swarms of flies. They splashed ponderously aside to let me pass, the stench of their hot breath heavy on the air. I searched the alder carr calling Lucy by name, but not a ripple moved and when I reached the open water meadows where the river runs deep between high banks overgrown with thistles, I gave up and turned back once more.

Jeanne was still sitting by the stream near the car patiently watching, but of Lucy there was no sign. It was as if the river had swallowed her. We stood talking, trying to bolster each other's failing morale, when I chanced to turn round and out of the corner of my eye caught a movement under the far bank where a ringlet of water stirred. Something had made it and it wasn't a fish. Slipping into the river I half swam, half waded beneath the bank, peering into the dark recesses hung with roots when Jeanne suddenly called 'There she is, behind you!' And there she was and furthermore there she had been all the time, lying up hidden at the back of the deep overhang, quite happy so long as she could hear one of us calling from time to time, telling her we were still around and all was well!

We were both so thankful to have found her we felt all our problems were solved, but they were not! Lucy, sensing the approaching dusk, had no intention of leaving the river and in the dark shadows of overhanging bushes she had only to remain still to become one with the dark water. Once, attracted by the towel Jeanne was holding, she followed her into the meadow only to wriggle free and dart back into the river before Jeanne could get a grip on her slippery fur. This was developing into a new game in which Lucy was master and she made the most of it, biting my hand hard enough to draw blood the only time I was quick enough to seize her in the water as she swam between my legs.

There seemed only one way of getting her back before night-fall and that was to net her, something we had never done to her or Kate, since we were afraid it would destroy their confidence. It was easier for me to keep contact with Lucy by staying in the water while she played around, so Jeanne drove home to collect Roy and the big catching net together with a large box trap four feet long for use as a last resort. She had been gone twenty minutes when I heard the car turn off the road and stop by the river in the usual place. Lucy heard it too and swam beside me as I made my way back. Seeing Jeanne on the bank she ran straight up to her and lay down to be dried on the towel, perfectly happy to be picked up and put in the car as if to show us we were making a fuss about nothing.

Lucy was even better than Fury for underwater filming once she had become accustomed to the bubbling of my aqualung and the glistening black wet suit. Sometimes she even made life difficult by sitting on top of my head in the water or resting her back feet on the camera casing while her head broke surface to look around.

Unlike Fury, who in the main ignored me, Lucy regarded me below the surface exactly as she did on dry land, a friend, protector and object of play, to whom she was proud to show her catch. Since eels were her favourite quarry this did much to help me lose my dislike of all but the largest, even when, in their first rush to escape her jaws, they mistook me for a rock and took refuge under my legs. Lucy always ferreted them out and I noticed that they soon tired, especially after she had caught them once and released them apparently without inflicting any injury.

Underwater, and seen in profile rather than from above, eels looked much more like silvery-green fish and less like water snakes. Sometimes Lucy seemed to drive one towards me quite deliberately as if hoping I would join in the game only to snatch it away in her jaws, twisting and spinning in a burst of silver bubbles before swimming up to the surface in search of somewhere safe to eat it. Often she chose a huge half-submerged tree, wedging herself between two jutting roots, her lower half still submerged and clearly visible to me, with the body of the eel hanging limply down. The rest of her had burst through the looking-glass surface of the pool into the sunlit world of men and I knew by the jerky movement of its tail that she had started to eat the eel.

8. Freckie and Kuala

So far as I am concerned there is one advantage to be gained from a long train journey – reading pages of the newspaper otherwise missed. So it was that travelling from Norwich to Bristol for a BBC television programme, I fell to studying the personal column of *The Times*, wondering vaguely what human unhappiness lay behind some of the pleas. 'Penelope please phone, three years, John, Reigate.' Was this testimony to unrequited love or criminal code for a bank robbery in Broadstairs?

One advertisement was plainly not in code for it read 'Film company has three otters for sale' followed by a London phone number. Only half interested, but since I was alone for the night in a Bristol hotel with nothing to do I sat on my bed before dinner and dialled the number. A woman's voice, high-pitched and aggressive, screamed in my ear 'Ottars, you must have the wrong numbar.' Slam. Re-reading the sequence I tried again, slowly and carefully, muttering the figures as I dialled them. Again the same piercing tones: 'Ottars, I've just told you, you've got the wrong numbar.' Slam.

Slowly the penny dropped – there must be a misprint, a phenomenon not unknown in newspapers. The three looked rather blurred, it might be an eight, so I tried that. This time a male voice 'Otters? I ain't got no otters mate. Try the bloody zoo'.

Was the nought rather small? Perhaps it was meant to be a six. I tried again. 'Who you say, Mr Otta? No I am sorry he is not available,' said an unmistakably Asiatic gentleman.

By now it had become a challenge. 1 was determined to crack the code. At the ninth permutation a male voice said 'Yes, we have three otters we were going to use in a film. I'm afraid I don't know much about them myself but I'll give you the phone number of the girl who is looking after them for us.

At the moment I believe they're being kept at Brighton Aquarium.'

'Can you tell me where they came from?' I asked, hoping to find out more about them.

'Yes, the producer went to Bangkok for them but unfortunately he was killed in a motor accident and as he was also the script writer the project fell through.'

So I knew the otters were Asiatic and likely to be smooth-coated or short-clawed. Asked about price the man replied that they hadn't much idea what tame otters were worth but thought a hundred pounds each would be fair.

Back in Norfolk I sent off the cheque and telephoned the number I'd been given.

Before his death David Rook had spent months taming the young otters which were to have featured in his film. Now his sister, Katie Rook, visited them every day and took the two tamest out for walks on Brighton beach. From her I learned there were two smooth-coated, a pair, and one female short-clawed. Of the smooth-coated the male, Oscar, was very tame and used to wearing a harness, while the little female short-clawed called Freckie was equally confiding and trustworthy.

All three otters had been kept together so when Katie Rook brought them to Great Witchingham a few days later I decided not to separate them but put them in one of our large breeding enclosures where they quickly settled in, enjoying the expanse of mown grass, the rock cave and den and the clear water of their pool. Soon their coats improved, acquiring a silken sheen when dry and breaking into spikelets the moment they left the water.

Mango, the female smooth otter, was the established boss of the group and while they lived in harmony, curling up together at night, I soon realized that though of different species, the females competed for the attention of Oscar, the male smooth-coated. At first I was afraid that Freckie might be hurt or even killed whenever Mango, consumed with jealousy, rushed at her, growling, to drive her away from Oscar. Sometimes the small otter made off, which quickly settled the dispute, but if Mango pressed home the attack Freckie rolled over on her back, an action which clearly inhibited the big otter from biting her.

Whenever he left the water it was always Freckie who waited on Oscar, throwing her fore-paws round his neck, nibbling and licking his fur while he lay on his side enjoying the attention. Mutual grooming is characteristic behaviour in otters, but it was interesting to see it carried on between individuals of such different species.

There was no doubting Freckie's devotion to Oscar and for the most part Mango accepted the situation. We used to take him out in the Park for an afternoon walk and on his return Freckie was almost hysterical in her greeting, rushing up to him literally screaming with pleasure, grasping him round the neck and nuzzling her nose all over his face and head.

Smooth-coated otters are large animals, the males often weighing well over twenty-five pounds against eight or less for a short-clawed. Their strong teeth with long canines are capable of inflicting really nasty wounds and coupled with a highly-strung, excitable temperament, makes them somewhat risky pets. Oscar was one of the exceptions and was the only otter I have known who would lie still and allow hordes of totally strange children to crowd round and stroke his fur. Not once did he show any sign of getting cross. Seeing me coming with his harness he lay flat on his belly, chin on the ground, and allowed me to slip it on, pulling each of his front feet through the braces in turn. He liked to be tickled, caressed, even rolled on his back, but any attempt to pick him up was always strongly resented with a threatening growl, starting on a low note, but quickly rising in volume and pitch. To have ignored this warning would have resulted at least in a lacerated hand and a loss of confidence on both sides.

Sometimes we took Oscar out for the afternoon to swim in the river. He was particularly fond of car journeys, jumping on to the front seat without any persuasion to lie across the back of it with his head out of the driver's open window watching the countryside fly by. At the river I took off his harness and let him go free. While a harness is acceptable on dry land it is little short of criminal to allow an otter to swim in one and I am horrified by the number of people who have done so. An otter can only hold its breath for two or perhaps three minutes at the most and a harness caught on an underwater snag invites certain death.

At first I was worried that Oscar might be difficult to re-capture, but so long as he was allowed what he considered to be time enough, he was never any trouble. Called, he followed me away from the bank and lay in the grass while I dried him on a towel and refitted his harness.

It is often possible to learn a great deal about wild animals by observing those in captivity which are allowed to live under semi-natural conditions, and this is particularly so in the case of such elusive and nocturnal creatures as otters. Up to that time very little work had been done on either the smooth otter or the short-clawed in the wild, and the newly-purchased trio taught me much.

Oscar, I found, was a natural fisherman, diving to catch roach and rudd with ease. Sometimes he came ashore to eat his catch, but more often he lay in the shallows holding the fish in his front paws while he ate it.

My other otters had all been content with the accommoda-tion we had made for them and I had taken care to install electric heating elements in the trio's den for use during the winter. Most otters dig a certain amount and the British otter is capable of burrowing up to a point, though rarely persever-ing unless there is a very good reason. Mango and Oscar soon showed me that smooth otters are born miners, capable of digging holts and tunnels that a badger might be proud of, nor did they require the incentive of a bank in which to start.

As in most matriarchal systems, Women's Lib was curiously absent. Mango did all the hard work, spending hours a day digging away with her front claws, reversing backwards from the tunnel dragging out piles of earth with her arms. Outside the entrance Oscar and little Freckie lay at ease in the sun. At intervals Oscar got up and went down the shaft to see how work was progressing while Mango was enjoying a brief rest. Once I watched him make a very half-hearted contribution to the digging, but he soon gave up.

Freckie was always delighted to see how things were going below ground, running in and out of the burrow humming to herself, sometimes taking tufts of grass down in her mouth as a help offering. The newly excavated soil intrigued her and she felt about in it until she found a tiny pebble, the size of a pea which, lying on her back, she juggled to and fro in her sensitive fore-paws.

Unlike the Indian otter which has large fully-webbed front feet with well-developed nails and even bigger webbed back feet, the short-clawed has five separate digits on all four feet, those on the front being joined by a vestige of webbing while the hind feet are about half-webbed. Each toe is soft, rubbery and rounded with a tiny nail or vestigial claw. So far as the front feet are concerned the result is a highly versatile pair of hands with mobile sensitive fingers.

The lack of webbing between the toes restricts the short-clawed's ability to swim though not enough to prevent it from catching small fish. Furthermore, its tail is rounded, unlike the smooth otter's powerful rudder, flattened and broad at the base, tapered as a sword.

Watching Freckie working with her hands I realized they must have evolved as a result of specialized feeding behaviour; then I noticed she rarely looked at what she was doing. If I threw a pebble into a shallow bowl of water she felt for it beneath the surface, at the same time looking around her with an air of concentration. If, as I suspected, her diet in the wild included tiny shellfish, crabs and other creatures, lurking beneath stones or in nooks and crannies, possibly in shallow, muddy water, there was the answer. The ability to feel for quarry while looking about obviously reduced the chance of a surprise attack by a predator.

One day, I thought, I shall go to some far-off Eastern land and put my theories to the test by watching both otters in the wild.

Tame otters often seem to have a natural aptitude for retrieving objects thrown by their owner and the reason, I think, is that they enjoy the game and are intelligent enough to realize that if they bring the object back it will be thrown again. Mango, I discovered, liked retrieving rounded pebbles about the size of a plum thrown into her pool. Watching my movements like a dog about to chase a ball she scampered away, dived into the water and reappeared with the pebble clasped firmly between one fore-arm and her chest, hobbling back on three legs. At the wire fence of her enclosure she sat up, took the pebble between her webbed fore-paws and threw or thrust it between the meshes into my waiting hands. Often she repeated this trick three or four times before tiring of it and sometimes, as if to show off, she swam the length of the pool balancing the stone on the crown of her head and she never dropped it before reaching land.

Soon after their arrival we gave all three otters a routine dose of worm powder as a precaution. Some weeks later Mango still looked rather thin and I feared she might be infected with microphilaria, microscopic worms which sometimes occur in otters and may be carried for years without seriously harming their host until they suddenly multiply rapidly and invade the liver, heart or lungs, resulting in death. The only cure is to give the powder 'Banacide' daily for at least thirty days. To ensure that Mango got her dose she had to be separated from the group and when Roy and I tried to crate her we found out just how loyal the otters were to each other. As soon as Roy rolled Mango up in the big catching net Oscar and Freckie threw themselves at him screaming with rage and as I ran to protect him with a broom they both turned on me. Luckily we got Mango into the crate and out of the enclosure before either of us got bitten.

At first we put her in the next door pen thinking she would prefer to be near the other two, but she spent a day and a night running up and down the dividing fence in a frenzy of hysterical screaming, which subsided only when we had moved her out of sight and sound of the others. Thirty days later we brought her back to a tumultuous welcome from Oscar and Freckie who went wild with excitement, both of them licking and nibbling her fur while Oscar held her face in his front paws.

It occurred to me that by separating Freckie there would be a better chance of Mango and Oscar producing a family, but such a move would result in far too much stress and unhappiness unless I could find Freckie a husband of her own species. For some months I scanned the animal dealers' price lists without success then, quite by chance, Ken Sims, who was managing a rubber estate in Malaysia, came home on leave and visited me at Great Witchingham. He was on the Executive Council of Kuala Lumpur Zoo and hearing I wanted a mate for Freckie remarked that they had a young male bred in the Zoo earlier that year.

On his return the Council agreed to send it to me in exchange for some waterfowl.

Kuala, as I christened him, was three-quarters grown and much smaller than his prospective wife for, unlike most other species, the female short-clawed is often larger and darker than the male.

As soon as he had recovered from the journey we put them together and the union was an instant success. Kuala seemed to regard Freckie as a substitute for his mother while she clearly looked on him like a long-lost son. To this day they are quite inseparable.

With the Eurasian otters breeding regularly, space was becoming a problem, so shortly before the British otters, Lucy and Kate, occupied the garden behind our cottage, we made the small garden at the front otter-proof and dug a pool for Freckie and Kuala, giving them a heated den beneath the apple trees.

The garden consists of a lawn above the level of the house running back from a low stone wall which borders a patio and paved path. Beyond the grass a wide shrub border curves round to give way to roses and herbaceous flowers with a clump of apple and plum trees to the right of the pool. For

Freckie and Kuala it was a dream home and they spent days sauntering round side by side like an elderly couple inspecting the flowers.

Jeanne is a keen gardener and she soon discovered she had a couple of enthusiastic helpers always ready to remove the rose from her watering can, unscrewing it with their hands and running off to drop it in their pool. Her rubber gloves disappeared the moment she put them down while the wet soil round newly-set plants proved ideal for sludging, most of the seedlings being uprooted in the process.

The crannies in the stone wall constantly aroused their curiosity and any small rock plant was soon found and extracted by their busy questing fingers.

Apart from minor nuisances they did remarkably little damage, never touching established plants nor digging to any extent apart from one favourite playground out of sight behind an old hedge of lilacs. Nor did they make any mess, since they always left their spraint in one particular spot behind their den where it was easily cleared up.

Always attracted by clothes hanging out to dry, Freckie's greatest joy was a new collapsible linen line which Jeanne had purchased. It is of the kind which stands in a socket set in concrete with four steel arms at right angles supporting the line. On a windy day the whole contraption spins like a roundabout and Freckie saw its possibilities at once, for a wind blew the first time it was put to use. Looking out of the window we saw her in mid-air whirling round and round hanging on by her teeth to one of Jeanne's skirts. Any garment within reach was likely to end up a sodden mess at the bottom of their pond.

If their garden enclosure was a source of new delights, the house was even more exciting when we opened the glass-panelled garden door to let them into the living-room in the evenings. At first they used to sit patiently outside twittering quietly to each other until one of us opened the door, but soon they thought up other ways of attracting our attention. Collecting a handful of small stones, they hurled them time after time against the glass panes, while Kuala found that a wet finger rubbed on the glass produced a squeaking noise that grated on our nerves so badly that we had to let them in.

Once inside the house Freckie was by far the more adventurous, making herself at home at once and quickly mastering the art of climbing the open staircase, something Kuala has never learned to this day, for his nerve always fails him on the third tread. Perhaps like me he suffers from vertigo. Upstairs, Freckie checks the bedroom doors and finding one open makes a nest of any clothes lying about, sometimes dragging them downstairs for Kuala to join in.

Living with us day after day both otters became remarkably confident and even Kuala lost his original reserve, though it is unwise to stroke him, for unlike Freckie who was hand-reared from a cub a few weeks old, he was brought up naturally by his mother. Familiarity has now replaced confidence to the point where they combine to remove anyone who happens to be sitting in their chosen chair and often as not when let in they rush first to the sofa or one of the armchairs, jumping up to roll and rub themselves dry on the cushions.

Like most animals, otters are quick to distinguish between people who like them and those that don't. Ignoring the latter, they tend to pester those they regard as friends. Kuala is not above giving a playful nip on the ankle to invite attention while Freckie always keeps an eye open for a jacket hanging over the back of a chair. In a matter of seconds her hands are deep in the pockets, fumbling and feeling through the contents for small objects likely to make good toys, often turning everything out on to the floor in her quest for a cigarette lighter or bunch of keys. Handbags she regards as treasure chests to be rifled, opening any clasp as quickly as a pickpocket. Lipsticks and fountain pens are the greatest prize, both of them likely to be damaged unless retrieved, for she treats them like sticks of rock to be held and chewed.

Often Kuala brings his own toys in from the garden. Usually they take the form of very small pebbles but sometimes he hobbles in carrying a worm, a special gift for Jeanne which he puts down reverently at her feet. He has never favoured me in this way, perhaps because I always have to throw Jeanne's worm back into the garden again.

There is one parlour trick we sometimes play on friends who are trying desperately and unsuccessfully to treat Freckie like a domestic cat. It always works for she cannot resist the temptation to drink water from a tumbler even when it is offered by a total stranger. Steadying the glass between her front paws she laps as delicately as a kitten, even allowing herself to be stroked at the same time, until suddenly, without warning, she plunges her head in and blows the rest of the water over the unsuspecting guest.

Neither Freckie nor Kuala has ever made a mess in the living-room and both are most punctilious about asking to be let out, squeaking at the garden door if the need arises. On the rare occasions when for one reason or another nobody has answered his plea, Kuala has always gone into the kitchen as if he knew the vinyl-covered floor was easier to clean up. Their curiosity is insatiable and they explore behind and under every piece of furniture. If the larder door is open and they happen to find a bucket of eggs on the floor, they bring one apiece into the living-room, holding it clamped to their chest in one arm, wobbling along on three legs. We have to move quickly to prevent an omelette on the carpet.

Hazel nuts are another favourite and Freckie has developed remarkable skill as a juggler. Lying on her back she can keep three nuts in the air together moving her little paws with the speed of lightning. Once she even managed to keep four going for a short time.

If Freckie had to choose her favourite place it would be our bathroom. The deep pile of the carpet is her idea of luxury while the bidet turned on fast enough to produce a little fountain is a never-ending source of delight. Standing on her hind legs she can just reach to dabble her hands in the jets or let them play on her face, always rubbing herself dry on the carpet before seeking some other diversion. She has a passion for warm water even if it does taste of Jeanne's bath crystals and likes nothing better than to stand on her hind legs holding the edge of the bath, which on tip-toe she can just reach, her mouth wide open to catch the water trickling from Jeanne's finger-tips.

Shortly after the otters took up residence with us our family was increased by one in the form of a European lynx cub which had been born in the Park. Three weeks old with her eyes just open, Grishkin was a round, speckled, fluffy ball of hissing fury, which had to be persuaded to drink milk from a bottle every three hours. From the start she was a rebel apparently set on a hunger strike.

With infinite patience Jeanne, helped by her daughter Gillian, gradually won the battle of the bottle, though not without hands raked and scarred by Grishkin's needle talons, for she only sucked if allowed to claw relentlessly with a kind of kneading motion at the hand holding the bottle. Cubs do much the same thing when suckled by their mother, pressing her belly each side of the teat alternately to stimulate the flow of milk just as a calf bunts its dam's udder. Only unlike Grishkin with a bottle they keep their claws sheathed. As she grew stronger Jeanne and Gillian had to wear leather gloves for protection.

Her diet of Lactol seemed to suit Grishkin although feeding her was always a messy business which meant washing her face and chest afterwards, something she detested. As with Lucy and Kate when they were babies we massaged her anal area with a wad of warm, wet cotton-wool to stimulate defecation after every feed.

By the time she was eating raw minced beef Grishkin had changed from a wildling to a docile household cat and the bigger she grew the gentler she became. Now her claws were kept sheathed whenever we played with her and if over-excited she chewed one of her own front legs rather than us. Compared with the otters her life was ordered by a set pattern of behaviour from which she never deviated.

Given a rabbit's leg she worried it, growling, and threatened us if we interfered, but at all other times she was more affectionate and playful than any domestic cat with a rasping purr like a lawn mower.

She had two disadvantages as a house pet, her extraordinary clumsiness, forever knocking things off tables and shelves, and her blank refusal to learn anything about being house-trained. Nothing we could think of seemed to make any difference and she could not understand being put outside when caught in the act. I began to wonder if she was possessed of some maniacal feline sense of humour for often she stopped playing and deliberately sat up to make a puddle in the middle of the living-room carpet, her round face grinning like the Cheshire cat.

It was still summer when Grishkin was old enough to spend the day in the garden with Freckie and Kuala, who from the start showed absolutely no fear of their strange playmate, rushing at her huffing and growling if she ventured too near their food bowls. The three of them played together by the hour with Grishkin stalking the otters, rushing out from the cover of the shrub border, often leaping right over them and delivering a playful tap with a paw in mid-air.

Most cats dislike water. Tigers are an exception for they love it and are strong swimmers. Our lynx drink a little but otherwise seem to regard their water bowl as a w.c. which we have to empty and refill daily. The first time Grishkin found the grass wet, she walked with mincing steps shaking each paw in turn, carefully avoiding puddles. But later she found a new game, running round the edge of the pool trying to swat Freckie or Kuala when they swam past. The otters were always too quick, diving a split second before the blow fell. In this way Grishkin got used to water and it nearly cost her her life.

The otters' pool is cleaned out every week and refilled from a hose, which takes several hours, largely because Freckie and Kuala will insist on bringing it out on to the lawn where they play with the jet, putting their paws across the end to squirt each other and often Grishkin as well when she used to join in.

On that day we had returned from shopping and I noticed the hose in the pool and the otters nearby, but no sign of

Grishkin so I wandered outside to look for her. The pool was only half full and in the deep end a very waterlogged Grishkin, her strength nearly spent, was desperately trying to get a grip on the steep and slippery concrete slope. Her paws found no purchase and her dog paddle strokes were getting slower. Throwing myself full-length I reached down, seized her by the shoulder and dragged her out. In a few more minutes she would have drowned. Most animals would have swum round the pool looking for a way of escape and had Grishkin made for the shallow end she could have walked out with ease.

After that episode I expected her to keep away from the water and always made sure she was shut in the house until the pool was full. But she swam more frequently, sometimes by mistake when she misjudged a flying leap at one of the otters. Brought up with them, I have a feeling she thought she too was an otter and did her best to be like them.

A hefty, clumsy, affectionate, half-grown lynx, Grishkin developed her own brand of humour often at the expense of our friends, some of whom were taken by surprise like two men who came to lunch. They both had beards and Grishkin was fascinated by hair in a place where she had never seen it before. I saw her eyes fix on the larger beard as she sank belly to the carpet and inched her way forward. Quite unaware, the owner of the beard, sherry glass in hand, was making polite conversation when Grishkin sprang, seized him round the neck with her paws and buried her teeth in his beard, purring in ecstasy. It says much for his nerve that he put down his glass without spilling a drop.

In the wild, lynx spend much of their time in trees watching for suitable quarry, often springing down to bowl over an unsuspecting bird or hare. For Grishkin the landing was an ideal vantage point on which she lay in wait for anyone coming upstairs. As they reached the bottom tread she dropped like a stone, sprawled across their shoulders, her face buried in their hair purring with delight. Caught napping it could be quite a shock.

She seemed to have a sense of the ridiculous in her clowning. One morning in late summer we were breakfasting in the garden and the wasps were being troublesome. I mistrust wasps and sat knocking them down with a fly swatter when Grishkin decided to join in. Jeanne recounts how she came out of the house to see the grinning form of the lynx riding pillion on my chair, its front paws wrapped round my waist batting down any wasps I missed which happened to pass her way, often with more success than I.

It was Gladys more than anyone who bore the brunt of Grishkin's tricks. She had worked for me for fifteen years and treated Grishkin with the same equanimity as she had all the other animals whether otters, badgers or bear cubs. But as Grishkin grew bigger I sensed that Glad no longer trusted her completely and the cat seemed to know and delighted in making her jump by springing out on her at unexpected moments. These attacks took place from behind, the lynx seizing her victim round the waist with her front paws. Once when Glad was putting something in the dustbin outside the kitchen, Grishkin was lying in wait eight feet above her on the garden wall. Just as she bent over the bin Grishkin dropped neatly on to her head and shoulders, her weight and the surprise combining to send them both sprawling. It took a stiff brandy to restore Glad's usual stoicism.

How Grishkin discovered that Glad wore bloomers I shall never know, but the result was disastrous, for the lynx added a new game to her repertoire. Waiting until Glad was busy cooking, with her back turned, Grishkin would choose her moment, then rush in, put her front paws up Glad's skirts and pull down her bloomers all in one split-second movement. The first time it happened we were so convulsed with laughter that despite Glad's shocked screams we were unable to move. Grishkin repeated this trick rather too often and from then on we took care to shut her outside when Glad was in the house.

Almost full-grown, she towered above the little otters and though she meant them no harm her games became too rough. Furthermore, she was able to leap the seven feet on to the top of the garden fence to terrify passers-by. We had no choice but to build her a new enclosure in a corner of the garden from which she could talk to Freckie and Kuala who paid frequent visits to their old friend. We still take her out for walks or have her in the house and to this day she has remained a great big, sloppy, docile cat who likes nothing better than human company.

Although Freckie and Kuala were a devoted couple, we held out little hope of breeding from them. Freckie was at least six years old and had never had a litter, while Kuala seemed to have little idea of courtship. Like other otters, Asian short-clawed mate in the water, the male gripping the nape of the female's neck with his jaws as the pair spin and roll together, often disappearing beneath the surface.

Kuala preferred to lie on his back on the lawn with Freckie on top and we felt this would hardly lead to consummation of their marriage. Of course what they did in the depths of their pool under cover of darkness was anyone's guess.

It was Roy who found the cubs one grey November morning when he came to the cottage to feed the otters. There were three, all of them dead, but apparently otherwise unharmed. Freckie had licked them dry, but was taking no further interest in them. Two of the babies were females and weighed 36 and 37 grammes respectively (about $1\frac{1}{3}$ ounces), the little male was smaller at 33·2 grammes (just over 1 ounce) and all were covered with pale grey fur. I was particularly interested to note that the male weighed less than his litter sisters at birth, for adult males are often the smaller of the sexes.

Naturally we were all disappointed and sad that her babies had died and we concluded that for some reason she had failed to feed them. Perhaps at her advanced age she had lost her maternal instinct. The den, with its electric heater, was warm and cosy and Kuala was obviously not interfering.

At seven o'clock that evening the two of them failed to put in their usual appearance at our garden door and when, an hour later, they were still absent, I decided to look in their box in case Freckie was ill. To my surprise and joy she had a tiny cub with her and it was alive. As I put down my hand to pick it up, Freckie rolled on to her side and I was able to pull her four teats gently in turn between my finger and thumb. She had not one drop of milk, which was clearly why the rest of the litter had died.

Removing the baby I took it indoors and showed it to Jeanne. Lying in the palm of my hand, its body, without the tiny tail, was the length of a matchbox and covered with very pale grey, velvety fur. It moved its limbs feebly and we could just hear its faint squeaks, for already it was weak from lack of food.

Jeanne decided straight away that she would hand-rear it, though the task appeared to me impossible with an animal the size of a mouse which had not had the benefit of the normal antibodies in its mother's colostrum. Having washed the glass dropper from an ephedrine bottle, Jeanne took the baby and dripped some warm Ostermilk into its tiny, pink mouth. She stayed up with it all that first night, giving it a few drops of Ostermilk every hour or so. Between feeds it lay on a clean tea-towel folded in the bottom of a plastic biscuit box, kept near the radiator for warmth.

To my amazement the cub was still alive next morning and seemed stronger. Perhaps there was a slight chance that we, or rather Jeanne, could rear it.

One of the first things we noticed was its paws, minute and rounded with a well-developed fine curved claw at the end of every toe like a European otter. The adult short-clawed, of course, has finger-like toes with only rudimentary nails, so here was a new discovery, or at least one which I had never seen mentioned in the scientific literature. It seemed to show that all otters had descended from a common ancestor relatively recently in evolutionary terms.

During the second day Jeanne persuaded the cub, whom we called Mouse, to take his Ostermilk from a human premature baby's bottle, though the teat was huge compared with his little mouth. He took about half a teaspoon every two and a half hours. We shared the night feeds and were so afraid we should not hear the alarm clock and oversleep that we got the telephone operator to call us throughout the night. At that stage one late feed would mean the death of the baby.

By the fourth day Mouse was taking up to one and a half teaspoons of Ostermilk every three hours and between feeds slept contentedly in his biscuit container next to the hot tank in the linen cupboard. We left the door ajar to make sure he did not suffocate.

Already his character was developing. When hungry or left alone he squeaked, a miniature version of the adult's call, but when fondled he twittered happily like a small bird and after each feed fell asleep in the palm of a hand, making tiny clicking noises of contentment.

Mouse grew remarkably quickly at first and by the time he was ten days old had increased his weight to 87 grammes (about 3 ounces). He began to slough a thin layer of dead skin starting from his nose and going over his head and down his back. It flaked off through his fur which appeared darker grey beneath.

At twelve days he was much stronger, taking up to two and a half teaspoons of Ostermilk every three and a half hours with a four and a half hour gap in the middle of the night. Placed on the carpet he was able to push himself in circles by his front feet, his rear end remaining on the same spot and his head, far too heavy for him to lift, recumbent on the floor.

By then feeding Mouse had become a routine. First we held him over the kitchen sink, gently massaging his anal region with a wad of warm, wet cotton-wool. This stimulated him to urinate and defecate. After feeding him we bathed his nose, which often became blocked with milk and mucus which had to be cleared. Finally, he had to be fondled and crooned to sleep.

When three weeks old he weighed 140 grammes (about 5 ounces) and took up to five and a half teaspoons of milk each feed, his little belly becoming so full that he took on the shape of an electric light bulb. We had thankfully cut out the night feed, Jeanne giving him one at midnight while I got up at six-thirty. Diurnal by nature, Mouse took little pleasure from this early feed, waking slowly with a series of subdued squeaks followed by yawns.

He was changing all the time and by then his eyes, which at eighteen days had just started to show as moist, dark slits, were about a third open. His claws had withered and several had already dropped off his front feet, while the pale colour of the lower half of his face contrasted with the deeper grey above. His nose had almost completely changed from pink to grey. He could crawl forward like a tortoise, taking very big steps on his tiny legs, but only as long as we supported his head.

Thin, black whiskers started to appear on each side of his muzzle when Mouse was a month old and a week later he cut his bottom canines. His eyes were fully open by then and he was able to hold up his head and crawl. All the claws had gone from his front feet.

By the time he was six weeks old most of his other teeth were through, and he moved his eyes as if beginning to focus. He weighed a healthy 340 grammes (12 ounces).

The Mighty Mouse was growing up fast.

Spurred on by what I had come to know of Asiatic otters in captivity I was determined to study them in the wild. Malaysia, with three resident species, seemed an obvious choice, more especially since both IUCN (International Union for the Conservation of Nature and Natural Resources) and the World Wildlife Fund were anxious to have more information on the status and distribution of all three otters in the peninsula.

9. Sampans and Sea Serpents

Anyone searching through the literature on otters will be struck by how little is really known about them in the wild. True of our own otter, even less is known about the lives of the tropical species. What little we do know has been gleaned from the casual observations of fishermen and big game hunters or from specimens kept in zoos.

Of the three species of otter inhabiting Malaysia virtually nothing was known about their distribution, the type of habitat each occupied, its food preference or its numbers. One professorial statement repeatedly quoted asserts that the hairy-nosed otter is 'abundant around Penang where as many as six could be seen besporting themselves in the sea'. Another says of the Indian smooth-coated otter that it is perhaps the rarest of the three in Malaysia and of the little short-clawed the accounts are even vaguer.

Was it really possible to see groups of hairy-nosed otters playing around in the sea in daylight? As far as I knew the hairy-nosed was as rare as its name was unusual. After much research I discovered that one had been kept for a time in New York Zoo, but of its life in the wild nothing appeared to be known and nobody could confirm the Penang story.

Despite its frustrations and discomfort, exploration of the wilder and more remote parts of the East has always fascinated me, and here was a chance to visit Malaysia and at the same time add something to our knowledge of three kinds of otter in one trip, the main purpose of which would be to gain as much information as possible to be presented in the form of a report for IUCN and the World Wildlife Fund. If the fabulous hairy-nosed really did abound anywhere and if the smooth-coated and the short-clawed really were largely diurnal the months ahead were likely to prove exciting beyond my wildest dreams. But somehow I felt there must be a snag somewhere; if not why was so little known and why hadn't somebody done it before?

The success of any field trip depends entirely on the extent and thoroughness of the ground work and planning done at home, long before anyone thinks of buying a pair of jungle boots. We were lucky in knowing Ken Scriven, the World Wildlife Fund representative in Malaysia, who lived in Kuala Lumpur and had years of experience in running wildlife safaris. Learning of our otter project Ken had written a letter to the *Straits Times* asking for anyone who had seen any otters anywhere to write to him with an account of their observations. This resulted in thirty-two replies from people of all kinds; university lecturers, Malay businessmen, Chinese shopkeepers, retired bank managers on the east coast and European rubber planters on the west. Many of the reports were vague: 'While driving from A to B at 11 p.m. an otter crossed the road and was seen in our headlights' or 'While walking along the beach four years ago two dog-like heads bobbed up in the sea, they were black otters.' Others were more precise: 'When riding my motor scooter from our village to the next at 3 p.m. last Saturday, I saw an otter run over by a scooter in front of me. I think it was wounded but it got away.' However vague such reports appeared, they established a general pattern which was to prove invaluable.

We decided to make the island of Penang off the west coast of Malaysia our first objective, for not only were we spurred on by the report of hairy-nosed otters but we were very lucky in having two contacts living on the island, both of them keen naturalists. Ken Sims had visited us in Great Witchingham some years before and had been instrumental in persuading the authorities of Kuala Lumpur Zoo to send us the little male short-clawed otter as a mate for Freckie. Now he was engaged on an ambitious project to set up a Zoo Park on Penang specializing in reptiles. Also living there was Bill Macveigh whom I had never met but we had corresponded and I remembered he kept otters and had hand-reared Freckie long before she came into my hands.

As our Boeing jet emerged from the cloud cover and began

its approach to the airport I got my first glimpse of the coast with its pattern of smaller islands and dark areas of mangrove swamp. If the otters live in there, I thought, how on earth are we going to find them?

Ken Sims, tall, blond and bronzed, was at the airport to meet us and it was typical of his cool efficiency that the first thing he did was to take us into the air-conditioned restaurant for an excellent breakfast of fried eggs and bacon and coffee, for we had left Kuala Lumpur at six o'clock that morning.

About fifteen miles long and ten wide, most of the built-up areas of Penang extend from Georgetown the capital, spreading southwards down the east coast and westwards along the north, ending with a chain of new tourist hotels at Batu Ferringhi. Inland the hills are covered with plantations and scrub while in the north there are still considerable areas of primary jungle. The climate, as all over lowland Malaysia, is very hot and very humid.

At Batu Ferringhi we met Bill Macveigh, even taller than Ken. Bill was in his early forties: bearded, tanned and dressed in immaculate white shorts and shirt, he reminded me at once of Ernest Hemingway. Born and reared in China, he had lived in Australia before finally settling with his widowed mother and sister on Penang. His bungalow was built on the banks of a freshwater creek, shaded by trees and within two hundred yards of the beach. In his large garden Bill kept his own private collection of animals, all of them delightfully tame and including an assortment of parrots, three pairs of gibbons and two pairs of short-clawed otters. Bill had decided to opt out of the rat-race of modern society and to spend his time studying wildlife. Fluent in both Malay and Chinese he had developed a relationship with the local people which was unusual for a European. Perhaps it was his understanding of people which enabled him to communicate freely with hippies of all nationalities who lived on the fringe of the tourist beat in spite of the government's efforts to bar them. Bill had even adjusted his life-style to suit the climate; rarely up before noon, he swam every day, worked at night in the cool, swam again in the early hours, retiring to bed around dawn.

He told us that a family of smooth otters sometimes came in from the sea and swam up the creek to call on his tame ones. Their visits took place at irregular intervals and always at night, though in the past when there was less disturbance along the shore they sometimes came in daylight.

In recent years the increase in the number of tourists combined with the activities of 'sportsmen' armed with ·22 rifles who shot at anything that moved, had driven the otters to a nocturnal existence, at least near human habitation.

One of the most promising reports and also one of the more recent had come from Gertak Sanggul, a fishing village at the extreme south-western tip of the island. We decided to spend a day following up the report and reconnoitring generally before attempting a serious search. As it happened it was a lucky decision for soon after we started the sky grew dark, the humidity soared to 98° and the heat was stifling. Then the rain came, so torrential that it was difficult to keep the car on the winding road as we crossed the hills on the way south.

Gertak Sanggul lay at the end of a rough track, a cluster of small houses and *attap* (palm) huts and the usual village coffee shop, open on all sides with an earth floor and a corrugated iron roof. We sat at one of the tables drinking thick sweet muddy coffee and eating coconut sweetmeats. A line of fishing sampans was drawn up on the beach behind the shop and a rather dirty freshwater creek five or six yards wide passed close by on its way to the sea. All the garbage from the café was tipped into this creek and while we were sitting there I saw a young water monitor swim downstream and climb out on the opposite bank.

Soon the locals, including the village policeman, began to gather, all curious to know what three Europeans were doing sitting in their coffee shop in the rain. Bill talked to the fishermen amongst them and asked them about otters. They said they knew the man who had sent in the report and it was true there were otters in the area – furthermore they often saw them. In fact they sometimes swam up the very creek by which we were sitting. After patient and prolonged questioning by Bill they admitted that 'often' was about three or four times in a year. But they knew of a man in the next village who had a tame otter which he had released and which still came back every night and slept under his hut.

The man with the largest boat, a diesel-engined sampan thirty-five feet long, wanted the equivalent of twelve pounds sterling to take us out for a day. Bill tried to beat him down without success. He then asked if we could hire one of the smaller boats, but was told they were not available as they were all fully occupied fishing. The man's argument was that he would miss a night's fishing by taking us out and a night's catch would be worth twelve pounds. As soon as they realized we were not going to pay so much they lost interest and wandered off.

We drove back the way we had come and stopped at the next village to enquire for the man who had the tame otter. It was a typical fishing kampong, a cluster of Malay houses built on stilts, most of them roofed with *attap* thatch, but some with corrugated iron and all shaded by coconut palms and only a stone's throw from the sandy beach where the fishermen moored their boats. Some of the houses were more affluent and had small gardens ablaze with purple bougainvillaea.

Nobody seemed to know about the man with the tame otter so we drove on to the much larger village of Telok Kumbar where Bill, bare-footed as usual, went into the local police station to make further enquiries. Jeanne and I sat outside in the car watching the muddy water swirling in the monsoon drains and listening to the rain. If we opened the windows we got splashed by the downpour and if we kept them shut it was like being in a Turkish bath.

We could hear raised voices from within the police station and a long conversation from which Bill learned that the police knew of the man with the otter and where he lived. It was true that it did come back every afternoon to play with him and furthermore they would telephone his village and send a messenger to warn him we were on our way.

Much encouraged we set off and found both the village and the man quite easily. He was Chinese and ran a small general store by the side of the main street, the usual open-fronted oriental shop with a concrete floor, built of timber and corrugated iron. Forty-gallon oil drums littered the entrance, and inside, the dingy building harboured a remarkable assortment of merchandise, smaller tins of oil, bailers and baskets made from the fibrous outer casing covering the young palm shoots. Two of these wired together with a rough wooden handle across the middle formed a serviceable bailer of the type used in every village household for throwing water over one's body in place of a shower.

At first the owner of the store denied ever having had an otter of any kind but soon the inevitable crowd of villagers collected and a Malay hearing his continued denials shouted out 'Of course he had an otter and it was stolen, everyone knows that.' The Chinese immediately replied 'It wasn't stolen at all, I let it go as everyone will tell you.' There followed a sustained argument amongst the villagers as to whether the otter had ever come back after its release, but the Malay still stoutly maintained that it had been stolen and sold to an animal dealer which seemed to me the most likely story.

In one thing we were successful, for a local fisherman offered to hire us his sampan for six pounds for as long as we cared to remain at sea and we arranged to sail with him in search of otters the next afternoon.

Returning to the small kampong the following day we waded out to the twenty-five-foot boat and loaded all our gear including cameras and a hefty earthenware barbecue oven complete with a bag of charcoal which Bill had brought along for a picnic, as we intended to be at sea for some time. It was all he could do to carry the oven which was about the size of a small barrel and must have weighed a hundredweight or more. Once aboard, the Chinese boatman swung the starting handle and reluctantly at first, the two-stroke diesel gradually came to life with its monotonous 'tonk tonk tonk', and we set off up the west coast of the island.

There was still a remnant of virgin forest on the extreme top of the ridge which ran parallel to the shore, but the slopes dropping to the sea were covered with scrub vegetation and patches of cultivation including many coconut palms which came almost to the water's edge leaving only a very narrow beach of smallish granite rocks. For the first two miles there were many kampongs and we passed fleets of small sampans fishing inshore.

The north-easterly wind whipped up a lumpy sea which became quite rough rounding the various headlands but the carvel-built sampan took it quite well as long as we were heading into the waves. Nonetheless, we shipped a lot of water which added to the discomfort of sitting on a pile of nylon fishing nets, for the tossing of the boat caused them to slither about so that we always seemed to be sitting on very hard warps or even harder marker floats.

Eventually we left human habitation behind, and rounding a rock-strewn point, came on a different coastline, for before us stretched ten miles of flat mangrove swamp which we were unable to approach owing to the low tide and extensive mud flats which kept us a mile or more out to sea. Birds were more numerous on this part of the coast, and we saw a pair of white-bellied sea eagles and several white-breasted kingfishers. Little terns were common and followed us, often diving close to the boat to snatch fry disturbed by our passage.

The monotony of the long stretch of mangrove swamp was aggravated by the necessity of using field glasses, though the chance of seeing otters through the heat haze at that distance was scant. Something much closer at hand provided welcome excitement for I suddenly spotted what I took to be a length of twisted rope, then realized that I was looking at a pair of five-foot sea snakes locked in a serpentine knot of nuptial embrace. We stopped the boat a few feet from them; they hung motionless a few inches below the surface so that we could see their flattened tails and pale grey bodies banded with black.

Sea snakes rarely attack swimmers unless provoked or disturbed when mating, but their bite is very poisonous, the venom belonging to the same group as the cobra only even more toxic and usually fatal unless the victim can be rushed to hospital for a shot of antivenin in time. When the sea is cloudy, as it often is in the Malacca Straits, bathers always run the risk of treading on a snake by mistake or even swimming into one.

Sea snakes have to come to the surface to breathe and are more active at night. Their teeth are so small that fishermen sometimes die from a bite without a mark being left on their rough weather-beaten hands or arms. The sinister sea serpent is surrounded by myth and if a fisherman dies from its bite his relatives usually refuse to admit it, or even to talk about it, for they fear that if they do, evil spirits in the form of sea snakes will attack and kill other members of their family.

Malays catching a sea snake in their nets invariably throw it back into the water alive since by killing it they believe that they or members of their family will be destroyed by the snake's relatives. Because the bite is often invisible they are convinced that if a man is holding the end of a net containing a live snake the venom will creep up the rope and into his body with fatal results. Their only cure for a bitten man is to make him drink some of the sea water collected in the boat's rowlock holes. This is done by soaking it up with a piece of rag and squeezing it into the victim's mouth. They also pour fresh lime juice on the bite in the hope that this will cure it.

By six o'clock in the evening we had cleared the mangrove swamp and once more the shoreline changed; the coconut palms had now given way to primary jungle guarded by wave-washed granite rocks, some twenty feet high, as we set a leisurely course for Pantai Kerachut. A few miles short of that place at about seven o'clock we were creeping along the shore forty yards from the rocks listening to the cicada chorus and the cries of jungle birds; the light was beginning to fade and I was just thinking that our chance of seeing any otters, other than by torchlight, was fast disappearing when Bill suddenly said 'Are those kra monkeys [the Malay name for crab-eating

8. Fury during filming on the Stiffkey marshes

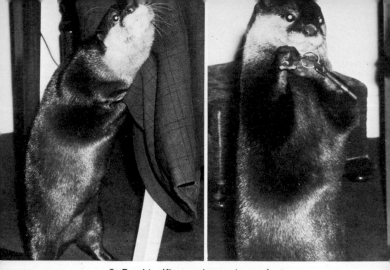

9. Freckie rifles pocket and gets the keys

10. Where does the water come from ?

11. Grishkin jumps over Freckie and Kuala

12. Freckie is displeased

13. The pitiful sight of a tethered otter at Potok Asam

14. Mango playing with a pebble

macaques] or otters on that rock?' My heart missed a beat and as always on such occasions it seemed ages before I could find the particular rock with my field glasses. When I did I saw to my delight a pair of smooth otters sitting side by side four feet above the water on a slab of rock, no doubt enjoying its warmth, for with the sun beating down on them all day the rocks act like night storage heaters. The boatman had cut the engine and as we drifted closer we watched as the otters got up in a leisurely manner. The larger male yawned and stretched, and then both slipped beneath the water. Though we waited for some time they did not reappear but the alarm calls of birds in the jungle immediately behind the rocks gave away their movements.

On the four-hour voyage back, the tropical moon rose full and round above the hills, the sea had dropped and a warm wind lulled us into snatches of sleep despite the hard nylon nets. Our wake was bright with luminous phosphorescence and sometimes the boat disturbed shoals of fry up to four inches in length which skittered about the surface like fireworks bursting in a shower of silvery-green sparks. Only the fear of sea snakes prevented us from heaving to for a midnight swim.

The coast from Telok Kumbar eastwards towards Batu Maung, though lacking jungle, is also inhabited by otters. The rocky strand backed by areas of cultivation with some extensive stretches of scrub provides sufficient shelter and seclusion especially where the coast road swings inland. A mile or two offshore lies Pulau Jerejak, a small jungle-covered island which was once a penal settlement. From there it is only a short distance to two more small islands, Pulau Aman, which means peaceful. The sea between them and the mainland is very shallow with extensive mud flats and creates no barrier for a powerful swimmer like the smooth otter, but probably accounts for the absence of the smaller short-clawed otter on the island.

Wherever primary forest remained there appeared to be a resident pair of sea eagles every five or six miles along the coast

and our observations, backed by very thorough questioning of
locals, especially inshore fishermen, led us to conclude that the
smooth otter had a similar distribution which would give a
total population of six to ten pairs for Penang and its offshore
islands. Young animals searching for their own territory
probably cross to the mainland and may have accounted for
several sightings on the Prai River estuary and in the neighbouring mangrove swamps.

One thing was certain, the elusive hairy-nosed otter did not
occur at all on Penang and almost certainly never had. Was it
to be found only in remote and uninhabited areas? Seventy sea
miles north of Penang close to the Thai border lies a group of
ninety-eight islands varying in size from sheer limestone
stacks crowned with a few sapling trees to others several miles
in circumference. All are uninhabited except the biggest,
Langkawi, which has a sparse population. To get there Ken
drove us ninety miles up the coast to Kuala Perlis, from which
small town we embarked on the local ferry for the twenty-
eight-mile voyage to Kuah, the only township in the archi-
pelago.

Township is hardly the right word, though Kuah is more
than a kampong for it boasts an ostentatious and expensive
country club said to be used as a retreat by tired Ministers.
There is also a government-run resthouse in which we stayed
and a single street some distance from the quay with the usual
open-fronted oriental shops. Cars are very scarce and only
one metalled road encircles the island.

We were interested in Langkawi because of two reports of
otters seen by a Chinese scientist, one of them near Sungei
Kechap at the sixth milestone on the road from Kuah to
Tanjong Rhu, a fishing village on the north coast, and the other
from Pulau Langgon, an uninhabited island of some size to the
north-east. While surveying on its shores Mr Wong Pak
Kheong, a government geologist, had seen two large dark otters
swimming in the sea. Were they perhaps hairy-nosed?

After two hours' sailing, the small ferry passed the first of
many islets of limestone or basalt, all with steep slopes and

covered with scrub jungle. There was very little life, probably owing to lack of both fresh water and fruit-bearing trees.

The arrival of the ferry was obviously the main event of the day for the inhabitants of Kuah, for at least three cars were waiting on the quay as well as a dozen tri-shaws and groups of shouting youths. We moored next to a patrol boat of the Malayan Navy and once ashore hailed two tri-shaws on to which we loaded our luggage. Bill rode in one and Jeanne and I in the other and despite their load the two men pedalled the mile to the resthouse in a surprisingly short time.

The European visitor to the island is immediately struck by the sheer limestone crags towering two or three hundred feet above the jungle, gaunt and grey, topped with delicate willowy saplings. Seen in the mist of early morning the stacks appear to rise out of the sea, reminiscent of Chinese landscape paintings, for this curious rock formation occurs not only in China but in a belt running southwards through Indo-China and onwards down the Malay peninsula. Transport might have posed a problem on Langkawi but for the kindness of the Indian manager of the rubber estate who persuaded a Chinese *towkay* (Chinese businessman) friend to lend us his ancient Austin Cambridge saloon which trundled along on bald tyres, its petrol pump apparently situated in the boot from whence its rhythmic beat sounded like a cross between a heart machine and a metronome, increasing in pace as the car gathered speed.

We drove to Kuala Teriang, a small fishing village on the shore, where we stopped for a glass of fizzy lemonade in the local coffee shop. The fishermen there said they saw otters from time to time both near Temonyong and further to the north.

In the heat of midday we stopped at Pasir Hitam where the long, deserted beach streaked with dark grey sand faded into a distant rock-strewn bay indistinct in the shimmering heat haze. At the other end of the beach a cluster of sampans rode at their moorings opposite the kampong where children played and shouted and turbaned fishermen squatted in the shade of the palms in endless confabulation while the womenfolk prepared their meal of rice and fish.

These people were part Malay and part Thai and regularly visited the Thai island and old penal settlement of Terutau twenty miles to seaward. They had no passports and considered themselves as much Thai as Malay. From them we learned that otters were often seen both in the rocky bay to the west and around Tanjong Rhu to the east.

After a picnic lunch of bread and peanut butter and bananas we swam in the warm sea which was comparatively clear with firm sand. Even so I must confess to a certain uneasiness for sea snakes were said to be common, not to mention very sharp-spined shells lurking on the bottom ready to impale the unwary. I also remembered the stonefish, so beautifully camouflaged as to be almost invisible even in clear water, whose sharp spines inject a venom which is nearly always fatal and for which there is no known antidote. In tropical seas it pays to keep swimming and to tread the bottom as little as possible.

Back in Kuah we ate a hearty meal in a Chinese restaurant, sweet and sour fish, prawns in butter and *fu hong hai* (crab omelette) and rice before Bill and I set off again for Tanjong Rhu intending to walk the beach until dark.

The silence of the deserted coast was broken only by the gentle threnody of the wind in the casuarina pines from which they get their local name of Rhu. The hot sand above the high water mark fried our bare feet, compelling us to walk in the shallows where shoals of tiny fish exploded across the surface.

Cuttlefish and coconut husks littered the strand along with man's debris which befouled even this unspoiled beach with plastic bottles and lumps of decomposing oil carried ashore from passing ships.

Kingfishers called from the scattered pines where one pair had a nestful of raucous young deep inside a hole in the main trunk. Solitary sandpipers tripped the tide edge and we found the tracks of domestic buffaloes, but no signs of otters. As the sun sank low in the sky we came to a deep inlet two hundred yards wide at full tide and beyond it the shore changed from wide expanses of sand to mangrove swamp backed by limestone cliffs. We were debating whether to swim across when a solitary sampan with an outboard motor came chugging by. We hailed it and the owner agreed to take us round the coast until dark for five Malayan dollars.

Having explored the inlet we turned back into the open sea and sailed up the coast towards a small island, passing a sampan under sail. The vessel was considerably larger than our craft and a whole family appeared to be living beneath the rough awning of coconut matting which served for a cabin. They were water gipsies, vagrants from Thailand, who spend their entire lives in their boats, living off the sea and wandering from coast to coast, claiming no nationality and ruled only by their own folklore and superstitions.

They throw nothing overboard for they believe that to do so would attract evil spirits in the form of sharks which would surely destroy them. All refuse including human excrement falls through the floorboards into the bilges and remains there until they decide to beach their boat to tip out the putrescent mess on to the shore. Our helmsman was careful to pass up-wind of the gipsy craft only to find they had chosen the island upon which we landed as their last dumping ground. Dense swarms of flies were already busy aiding the process of putre-faction. Beyond the island we entered a much larger inlet, or sound, with thick mangrove swamp on the west side and sheer limestone cliffs on the east, the latter riddled and honeycombed with caves, grottoes and fissures running far back into the darkness forming remote caverns with dry shelves and beaches, almost any of which would have provided a safe retreat for otters.

We sailed right up the inlet along the edge of the mangrove swamp turning back down the eastern shore and keeping close in beneath the cliffs while we scanned the rocks with binocu-lars. Regaining the main bay we turned east along the same range of limestone cliffs covered in thin jungle rising up to one thousand feet, honeycombed with caves and interspersed with tiny beaches. In a much larger mangrove area we came across the only other craft we saw that evening, a sampan with two fishermen moored against the edge of the swamp. One of the men spoke fair English which was so unexpected we asked him where he had learned it.

'At school in Kuah,' he replied, 'but I don't get any practice.' Then almost as an afterthought, 'And I can speak little French as well.'

That Malaysia has spent vast sums of money on schools in even the most remote rural areas is at once obvious to any visitor. It was perhaps characteristic of the Malays that this young man, despite his education, preferred to remain on Langkawi and live exactly as his forbears had done for generations. From him we discovered that otters were often seen in and near the mangroves and furthermore he claimed that three otter cubs were for sale in his village at Potok Asam on the road to Kuah.

'Come tomorrow morning early,' he said, 'and stop at the coffee shop beneath the rambutan tree near the 16¼ milestone and I will show you.' We assured him we would be there.

The following morning the three of us drove to Potok Asam where our fisherman was waiting outside the coffee shop, an open-fronted tin-roofed shack in the shade of a rambutan tree, just as he had described.

He led us along a path beneath the coconut palms and across a wooden plank bridge over a large irrigation canal, towards a cluster of *attap* houses amongst the trees. Outside one of them, close to the canal bank, a young and very thin smooth otter was tethered by a long cord tied to a piece of wire twisted tightly round its neck. A few yards of sun-baked earth separated it both from the shade beneath the house and the cool water of the canal, neither of which it could reach. The otter was obviously suffering from malnutrition and probably from hook-worm which occurs in wild otters in Malaysia as well as in humans. It belonged to one of the sons of the house, a lad of twelve who refused to sell it but told us that he had parted with the other two, a pair, only the day before to a Chinese in Tanjong Rhu for $25 the two.

As we returned across the wooden bridge I looked back

towards the house and saw the pathetic figure of the little otter sitting upright, straining at the limits of its tether watching us go. I knew it could not survive such harsh conditions for more than a few weeks and hoped that it would soon find release in a painless death.

The Chinese had a house-cum-office beneath a clump of palms on the sand dunes just outside Tanjong Rhu where a woman, probably one of his wives, managed the anchovy drying business upon which the village, with its trawler fleet, depended. She showed us the two otters tied together, their tethers all twisted up, hiding under an upturned wooden box, but said she had no authority to sell them and we must ask their owner who was at his house in Kuah.

Back in the town we were lucky to find the man at the one and only petrol pump and after much bargaining Bill purchased both otters for $50 and the man came with us to buy a small laundry basket in which to carry them.

Returning to Tanjong Rhu our first thought was to cut off the dreadful wire collars and since the Chinese was afraid of the otters, I grabbed one and held it while Bill struggled to get the pliers between the encircling wire and the animal's neck. He succeeded after some difficulty and I popped the otter into the basket which we had lined with a plastic macintosh. It was soon joined by its sister and we set off once more for the rest-house at Kuah to pack our belongings.

Before we left Penang, Bill had arranged for us to be picked up by a light aircraft from the flying club which was to take us back that afternoon. The plane would reduce a day's travel to little over an hour which would be far better for the otters and meant they would be safely in Bill's garden by early evening, for he had agreed to care for them until after we returned to England to fix up quarantine and other formalities.

The Indian manager of the rubber estate took us in his Land-Rover to the abandoned air-strip in the west of the island which had been built just after the war for a commercial service which never materialized. We waited for the plane in the 'airport lounge', a rectangle of concrete surrounded by a low wall just high enough to sit on in comfort and warm to the touch even in the shade cast by the coconut palms. At one end a gap in the wall enabled passengers to walk out to the strip, at the other stood the semi-derelict booking office, its shutters swinging in the breeze, and the abandoned lavatories with broken doors and a litter of rubbish on the floor. Half-way down the runway a wind sock hung limply from its pole, stirred by fitful gusts, boys rode bicycles up and down the concrete and buffaloes chewed the cud in the shade of the surrounding trees or wandered casually across the landing strip.

A few minutes after four o'clock we spotted the plane coming in high over the forested hills. Passing overhead it disappeared beyond the trees and a few minutes later we watched it coming down at a steep angle at the far end of the runway. As it taxied to a halt a few yards away it looked even smaller than we had imagined.

Charlie Downs, the cheerful Australian pilot, was not in the least put out by us, the amount of luggage, or the fact that we had two live otters in a laundry basket. Jeanne and I climbed into the back seat and Bill passed me the basket which we managed to squeeze in on to my knees. Despite his height Bill somehow folded himself into the front seat beside the pilot.

At the end of the strip the engine roared into life and waving to the onlookers, we quickly gathered speed. Just as I felt we were about to lift I heard the pilot say 'Not enough power for that kind of take-off'. The trees at the far end of the runway seemed perilously close as the plane slowed down, turned and taxied all the way back, much to the surprise of the estate manager and the boys who were still there.

For the second attempt we started on the grass beyond the strip; gathering momentum, the Cessna's tail lifted and wagged from side to side as we became airborne, soaring up over the trees and turning left over the sea. As we crossed the hills the little plane bounced and swayed in the thermals but settled down as we climbed to 5000 feet over the water. Below and to the left we could see Kuah and the country club, to the right Pulau Dayang Bunting, a largish island with forested mountains and an area of mangrove swamp separating it from neighbouring Pulau Tuba. Out beyond Kuah a pattern of islands and stacks spread across a sea so blue that it matched the sky and swallowed the horizon.

Our trip had provided us with evidence that the smooth otter was well distributed on the Langkawi group of islands, as well as on Penang. But was it always a coastal species or did it also live in the main river systems of the interior?

To find out we decided to visit Malaysia's most spectacular wildlife reserve on the Tembeling River. Originally called the King George V but now renamed the Taman Negara National Park, it extends to 1677 square miles of steep mountains clothed with tropical rain forest so dense that it is almost impenetrable. There are no roads in the Park and the only access is by way of the river. The vast area of the interior is uninhabited save for a few tribes of wandering aborigines and only properly organized and equipped expeditions can penetrate its remoteness.

Ken Scriven had arranged for us to spend a week at a lonely forest resthouse in the interior, sixty-seven miles upstream from the point of embarkation at Kuala Tembeling, a small riverside kampong with little to offer but a wooden jetty.

Our party had been increased by two new members, Robin Chancellor, an old friend and keen naturalist who had just flown out from England to spend a month otter-searching with us and Soo Keat, a young Chinese bird artist who was to act as interpreter, being fluent in Chinese and Malay as well as English. Slight of build, with glasses and always immaculately dressed in flared, neatly laundered jeans and flowered shirt, Keat's looks concealed a character that combined toughness with remarkable tolerance and made him the perfect dragoman.

The boat waiting at the jetty to take us up river to Kenyham was about twenty-five feet long, very narrow in the beam, shallow in draught and with its long slender pointed bow resembled a war canoe. It was crewed by two Malay boatmen who were to remain with us throughout the trip. Powered by a 40 h.p. Johnson's outboard motor, the boat surged along at a good twelve knots, and after two hours we reached the entrance to the National Park where the jungle proper began, a green sea sweeping to the edge of the sixty-foot high banks. Four hours and three sets of rapids later we rounded a bend between wide sandbars and caught our first glimpse of the lonely resthouse at Kenyham perched high above the river in a jungle clearing.

The following day we examined every sand-bank below the resthouse and were soon rewarded by the fresh tracks of at least six smooth otters leading from the water's edge up to a sprainting place on the top of a sandbar.

The otters appeared to be going downstream and we found their tracks on almost every stretch of sand. Suddenly Osman, one of the boatmen, pointed excitedly to a place on the opposite bank exclaiming '*Barang, barang*!' For a moment I thought he had actually seen otters, then I saw a maze of otter tracks leading up the sandy bank to a level place twelve feet above the water. From there the animals had made a slide which was what Osman had first noticed. Landing, we found a large area of very fresh spraint beyond the top of the slide and feeding on it a black butterfly with lime green ovals on each wing, a Malayan Nawab.

After photographing the slide and the tracks, I took samples of spraint and we returned to the boat highly delighted for it was almost certainly the first time anyone had photographed such a well-used slide made by smooth otters in the wild.

We soon developed a daily routine concentrating on the six-mile stretch of river below the resthouse. Every morning we left before sunrise and drifted in silence down the full six miles, landing on every patch of sand to check for tracks and spraint. As we were carried downstream we listened to the jungle waking up as the light increased. First the Argus called from the hills, then the yellow-crowned bulbul warbled its mellifluous song. At first light a white mist lay across the high ground, hornbills cronked as they flew in search of ripe forest fruit and as soon as the sun rose above the mountains and bathed the tree tops in its warmth the white-handed gibbons welcomed the new day with a chorus of whoops, one troupe answering another like distant crowds cheering at a football match. As the heat increased the cicadas began until their concerted din drowned all but the loudest noises.

The late afternoon found us on the river again drifting downstream watching for otters, and only returning when just enough light remained for the men to negotiate the rapids and for Osman to see and fend off drifting timber.

Slowly we were able to piece together the otters' nightly activity. We found two more slides, neither of them as high as the first, but both leading down to the water from sprainting places on top of high sandbars. We discovered where the otters had dried themselves, where they had played games, chasing each other about on a wide flat beach of rippled sand. We saw where they had brought fish ashore to be eaten, though they rarely left more than a patch of fresh scales.

One morning we found a small sandbar criss-crossed with fresh tracks all round a sprainting place, leading along the water's edge towards a small side stream which ran back into the jungle between high rocky banks overgrown with dense vegetation. In the middle of the mouth of the stream a patch of exposed mud also had tracks leading into the jungle. It seemed that our chance to waylay the otters when they set out for their night's fishing had come at last. Jumping out of the boat I splashed water over the mud and smoothed it with my hands, for I was determined to keep watch for the otters that night. If they left the stream before our return we should know, for they would certainly cross the piece of mud.

Before leaving, Keat and I waded up the stream for about a quarter of a mile. There were otter tracks wherever there were patches of mud but we lost them when the bed of the stream became stony. The bottom varied from a foot of soft mud with sharp stones and boulders underneath to gravel and rocks with frequent fallen trees barring the way, some of them palms with needle-sharp thorns all down the sides of the leaves as well as a mass of vicious spikes all over the stem.

At half past four that afternoon we all set off in the boat,

Jeanne and Robin dropping off Keat and me near the stream while they went to catch some fish for supper. The boatmen were to return to collect us as late as the light permitted.

Not far from the mouth of the stream a large slab of rock lay at a steep angle against the edge of the jungle and from the top of it we could keep watch over the whole area below while remaining well hidden. The continual purling of the water tumbling over a small rapid at the end of a rocky promontory drowned any noise we made.

While we waited, lying side by side on the rock, our field glasses ready, spine-tailed swifts hawked flies up and down the river. As they swept past we could hear the clicking of the echo location system which enables them to beam in on their quarry, as well as to find their way in the dark caves where they roost. The light seemed a long time going and there was little to watch apart from a pair of rhinoceros hornbills which landed in a tree quite close to us. There was little birdsong and in the western sky dark thunder clouds began to build up. At six o'clock the first drops of rain fell, to be followed by a torrential downpour. We hid our field glasses and cameras in the dry beneath an overhanging slab of rock and returned to our vantage point. In a matter of seconds we were soaked to the skin, the cold water sluicing down the surface of our rock and the rain beating mercilessly on our bare backs. For the first time in weeks I began to feel cold and wondered if it was all worthwhile. Twenty minutes later the rain eased, eventually stopping, and at half past seven when it was almost pitch dark we heard the boat returning. On the way back we shone our powerful torches on both banks hoping to catch the reflection of otters' eyes, but apart from a startled civet cat scavenging on the shore we saw nothing. Next morning fresh tracks across the small island of mud and on the shore showed where the otters had left the stream later in the night.

Our daily patrols confirmed that one family party of six smooth otters were more or less permanent residents of that particular stretch of river at that time, though this did not prevent other otters passing through. One morning we found a different set of tracks made by an adult pair moving upstream through our area, possibly in search of a suitable breeding territory. Some of the tracks were exceptionally clear and I noticed that when an otter was loping along quite fast, almost at a canter, the large hind feet landed six or eight inches in front of the prints made by the fore feet with a gap of about a yard before the next two prints made again by the fore feet. The European otter moves in a similar way but with shorter gaps between the prints.

One night there was an unusual amount of otter activity along our beat. Next day almost every sandbar we examined was covered in otter tracks, some moving up river, some down, and it became apparent that two more groups had passed through the area the previous night. All the usual sprainting places high on the sandbars or banks had been visited, resulting in exceptionally large quantities of fresh scats, most of it containing distinctive scales of cyprinids (fish of the carp family). The Malay Nawab butterflies and *Dysphania militaris*, a gaily-coloured day-flying moth, were having a rare feast on the fresh droppings.

Two out of the three slides had been used, one of them for the second night running and we concluded that at least fourteen and possibly as many as eighteen otters had been active in the area and for part of the time had moved and fished as a single group. The following night, things returned to normal with only the tracks of the resident family showing in the morning.

The young of the smooth-coated otter, like those of the European species, develop slowly and probably remain with their mother for nearly a year. During this time it seems likely that the male also stays with the family and that the group only breaks up when the youngsters are old enough to fend for themselves and the adult pair are free to breed again. The sociability of the species and the mixing of family groups reduces the likelihood of inbreeding and helps to maintain the population at an optimum level.

With no persecution and so little disturbance, I was surprised how nocturnal the otters of the Tembeling River were, but the boatmen told us they were seen much more often during the height of the hot season when the small streams in the jungle dry up and the midday heat forces the otters to leave the shelter of the jungle and come down to the main river to cool off in the water. We had been told that the smaller Asian short-clawed otter also lived in the National Park. While it may occur in some of the small streams in the lower valleys, it is certainly not found in the main rivers, for the two species rarely, if ever, occupy the same habitat; so to see the short-clawed we had to search the swamps and paddy fields of the east coast.

10. Coconuts and Coral Reefs

The east coast of Malaya fulfils everyone's dream of a tropical shore: long, curving, empty beaches of white sand shimmering in the heat haze, tiers of creaming surf on a blue sea and a backdrop of coconut palms with here and there a wooden house on stilts. Nowadays a road runs the length of the peninsula keeping close to the sea from Singapore north to Kota Bharu and beyond.

The coastal plain is quite narrow with jungle-covered mountains never far inland and while most of the numerous rivers have been bridged, some still have to be crossed on raft-ferries which cannot operate during the monsoon when the region is cut off from the rest of the country.

As we drove through the mountains from Kuala Lumpur to Kuantan, the only town on the east coast between Trengganu in the north and Singapore in the south, I wondered how the next three weeks would unfold and what, if anything, they would produce in the way of otters. With over two hundred miles of coastline, not to mention rivers, paddy fields and mangrove swamps, where should we begin to look for them? We had two or three possible contacts gleaned from the list of people who had sent reports of otter sightings to Ken Scriven. One from Kuantan appeared on paper to be extremely promising. A young Chinese lad had written in fluent English that he would be delighted to act as our guide, that he knew the area like the back of his hand, especially the wilder parts to the south, and was a keen naturalist with an ambition to work for the World Wildlife Fund. What better recommendation?

It was some time before we located the boy's house on the outskirts of the town and then he was out fishing, but his father assured us he would come to our hotel later that evening. In due time he arrived. Now I was half expecting what might perhaps be best described as a 'likely lad' and was quite unprepared for the enormous, ebullient, fat and, even for a Chinese, over-confident youth who immediately ordered a round of beers, and suggested above the incessant noise of piped Chinese music that we should have something to eat as well. Yes, he was certainly interested in natural history, thought of nothing else in fact, and his father was very keen for him to get a job with the World Wildlife Fund. As he ladled more food on to his plate I guessed his father would be only too glad if he got any kind of job. Since he had heard about us from Ken Scriven he had spent weeks searching for otters, indeed only yesterday he had actually caught a half-grown one and had been badly bitten, as his bandaged hand testified. I felt he had more likely cut it opening a can of beans. His father (whom we had met and who was a small-time shop-keeper) was a man of influence and had already written to the Prime Minister requesting the co-operation of the entire forest department in our survey. Dollars, lots of them, were clearly his main interest and with all the signs of a budding entre-preneur I was sure he would end up a tycoon, but clearly we could not afford to feed him, apart from anything else.

One piece of information which the boy let slip proved very valuable for he mentioned the name of a major in the Army who lived in Kuantan and was a very keen big game hunter. We found the Major's home the next morning and over coffee he listened to our problem. He had spent most of his spare time hunting in the mountains and had shot his last tiger only eighteen months before. Now he was rapidly becoming more interested in watching and conserving wildlife than in killing it and was particularly concerned at the virtual disappearance of the magnificent green peacock which used to be common in the area. He had often seen otters but had not taken particular note of them though he was aware of the difference between the large smooth otter and the small short-clawed. More important he had two friends who were both knowledgeable about wildlife and who lived in areas where otters were common. One, Aw Joon Wah, lived at the mouth of the Kerteh River near Dungun to the north and the other, Mr

Koo, was the bank manager in Rompin, a large kampong to the south. To both of these gentlemen he gave us letters of introduction.

As the road south approached Rompin it passed through a remote and desolate area of scrub jungle and scattered plantations, finally reaching the banks of the Rompin River which had to be crossed on a steel raft, carrying up to half a dozen cars, the somewhat primitive contraption being hauled to and fro by cables operated by a diesel-driven winch.

The town, for Rompin almost deserved that title, consisted of a long, narrow main street lined with shops and crammed with people, bicycles, wandering cows and goats and a few cars. On either side of the road a labyrinth of alleyways connected rows of houses and shacks. Only the main road boasted a tarmacadam surface, the rest being dirty sand-tracks or footpaths.

The bank, a small building, cool and gloomy, was right in the middle of the town. One of the two clerks ushered us into the manager's office where Mr Koo, bespectacled and urbane, with the slanting eyes and high cheek bones of the Oriental, sat behind his desk apparently studying a single sheet of paper. The clerk brought in four chairs for us which completely filled the room and Mr Koo, having signed the piece of paper, took our letter of introduction without a word and read it. In hesitant, but otherwise excellent English, he said he would come to the resthouse in an hour's time and would bring with him his assistant who would be able to help us.

The resthouse was a mile out of the town and had been built only a year ago, so that it was almost luxurious with electric fans which worked and outside a hard tennis court which no one seemed to use.

Mr Koo's assistant was not, as I had imagined, connected with the bank but seemed to organize a number of other business sidelines, one of them a farm growing melons. It is never easy for a European to judge the age of a Chinese who is neither very young nor obviously old and Ah Fatt, who spoke no English, appeared to be in his late forties. It soon became apparent that he was a man of tremendous energy who knew everyone and everything in Rompin and I have no doubt his knowledge was helpful to Mr Koo in the bank, though as the latter explained:

'Nobody in Rompin has any money so there is very little banking to do. I applied for a transfer three years ago but it has not come through yet. I don't mind it but my wife doesn't like it. There are no good shops and the food is poor, there is nothing to do in Rompin.'

From Keat we discovered that Ah Fatt was once well off but gambling and women had been his downfall. He seemed to have tried his hand at almost everything and had spent a spell in hospital after damaging his back by falling from a palm tree when picking coconuts.

After an early dinner at half past six, Keat and I set off with Ah Fatt, who was confident he could show us some otters. Rather to my surprise we found ourselves on the side of the main road a mile to the north of the ferry. The area was low-lying with scrub jungle and on one side a semi-derelict rubber plantation, while on the other a deserted house was surrounded by an overgrown palm grove. Both verges were lined with bushes rather like oleanders, and parallel with the road on both sides was a shallow, muddy dyke full of water lilies and smothered by dense vegetation. At intervals other ditches led off into the darkness of the trees.

According to Ah Fatt this was the best place to see otters and we would surely be successful. On our first night in a new area it seemed too much to hope. For an hour and a half we kept constant watch on both sides of the road; half a moon rose above the palm trees, the heavy night air was full of the whine of mosquitoes and the long-tailed nightjars kept up their monotonous 'teonk-teonk'. A procession of timber lorries roared past, each carrying half a dozen huge trunks of hardwood to the local sawmills. I wondered how long the jungle could stand plundering on such a scale. Of otters there was no sign.

Another car pulled up and Mr Koo got out with two Chinese friends. Standing in the middle of the road they carried on a seemingly endless conversation with Keat and Ah Fatt at the top of their voices, only stepping aside at the last minute to avoid the timber lorries hurtling through the night. I gathered they were discussing all the otters they had ever seen and judging by their gesticulations each claimed to have seen the biggest.

Eventually the party broke up and Ah Fatt disappeared in the darkness.

'Where has he gone?' I asked Keat.

'He's walking back to the ferry to buy some cakes in the coffee shop because he's hungry,' came the reply.

Returning to the car I sat on the bonnet, smeared more mosquito repellent on my face, neck and arms and despite the stifling heat, dozed. I was awakened by Ah Fatt's return and the ensuing shouted conversation with Mr Koo and his friends. Then it all stopped and Ah Fatt walked past the car. Jumping to my feet I followed a few paces behind him, stopping whenever he did to listen for otters. My long trousers worn as protection against the mosquitoes were intolerably hot and the fireflies dancing before our eyes were like liver spots during a bad hangover. Suddenly Ah Fatt froze, listening, then moved cat-like to the water's edge. Following, I could hear rustling in the vegetation which grew right over that part of the dyke. Squatting down, Ah Fatt listened and again we heard the rustling a few yards on our right. Putting his hand in the water he imitated the splashing of a fish stranded in the shallows. The rustling increased and then I heard the subdued bird-like twittering which I knew at once was the contact call of a pair of short-clawed otters chattering to each other as they sludged in the water beneath the canopy of vegetation. For perhaps five minutes the noise continued then we noticed the moonlight flickering on ripples spreading across a path of open water in front of us. The otters were less than five yards away and I felt sure they must hear us breathing. Something moved beneath the far bank and Ah Fatt suddenly switched on his torch. Caught for a moment in its beam the two little otters looked surprised then both dived and disappeared. Seconds later we heard them moving up one of the ditches leading back into the scrub and although we waited for another half-hour we saw nothing more.

On the way back to Rompin Ah Fatt told Keat he knew of a man in the town with a pet otter which we could buy and he promised to take us to him the next day.

The following morning we met once again in Mr Koo's office. After sitting in silence for a while, Ah Fatt got up and went outside, returning later with bottles of 7-Up which he distributed. Every time we heard a car approaching he rushed outside. Puzzled by his behaviour, I asked Keat what was happening.

'We are waiting for the man with the otter,' he replied.

A customer came into the bank and both Mr Koo and Ah Fatt had a long conversation with him after which Ah Fatt left, beckoning to us to follow. It appeared that he had given up the first man with the otter and was now taking us to another man who lived in a shack on the shore of the estuary and was said to have an otter cub. After a great deal of questioning and visiting different homes and shacks we found the family with the cub, only to learn it had died a week before. However, there was another belonging to a man living in a house amongst the palm trees nearer the sea. We set off again down more hot and smelly alleyways of dirty sand, hordes of flies buzzing round our faces, until we reached the house, but the otter had already been sold and had been taken to Kuantan the day before. Back to the town for more 7-Up.

At length an old Mercedes drew up and a Malay joined us and sat talking to Ah Fatt until eventually we all piled into the Mercedes and were taken to the man's house on the outskirts of the town. In the backyard, tethered to a root of a tree, was a very small short-clawed otter which I estimated to be about four months old. Its head appeared too large for its tiny body and with its pot belly and dry staring coat it looked pathetic. There was a small wooden hutch into which it could crawl for shade and half a coconut shell into which members of the family poured water whenever they remembered. We were told they fed it on cooked fish in the curious belief that this would make it so dependent on them that it would never run away, though how it could ever escape from its tether I failed to understand. When I tried to pick it up it huffed at me and rushed beneath its hutch whereupon one of the children dragged it out by its tether.

Keat explained that the Malay was a local businessman of substance who would take offence if we offered to buy the otter, but Ah Fatt was telling him all about us and our interest in otters and why we were in Rompin. This softening up would go on for two or three days then Ah Fatt would give a present of fifteen or twenty dollars to each of the man's children, then perhaps he would offer to give us the otter. As we left I hoped it would survive the next few days.

Although Keat and I, sometimes joined by Robin or Jeanne, kept a dawn and dusk watch on the dykes beyond the ferry for several days, we saw no sign of the otters but were told that the men building the new bridge across the river had killed several with iron bars and stones.

Mr Koo and Ah Fatt seemed genuinely upset at our lack of success and volunteered to take us one evening to a new place south of the town. This was a long freshwater lagoon a few hundred yards inland from the seashore from which it was separated by a belt of casuarina pines and scrub jungle through which ran an overgrown earth embankment or 'bund'. The lagoon, nearly half a mile long and a couple of hundred yards wide, had small clumps of palms forming islands and apparently was a favourite place for otters. It was here that the cub we had seen had been caught.

After watching for two hours we had seen nothing – only rising fish disturbed the placid water. The men had a discussion and Ah Fatt went off to Mr Koo's car returning with a casting net. When laid out flat the net was circular in shape and weighted all round the perimeter with a light galvanized chain. A length of rope was attached to the centre of the net; coiling this and the net carefully in his left hand, Ah Fatt waded out into the lagoon. A few yards short of the nearest shoal of rising fish he stopped, and with his right hand began swinging the weighted end of the net round and round his head. Suddenly he let it go and the net sailed out over the water forming a perfect circle in the air before landing, evenly spread, over the shoal. As Ah Fatt drew it slowly towards him, the weighted hem closed up trapping eight catfish and one snake-head. Considerable skill is required to throw one of these nets, which are used by fishermen all along the east coast for catching mullet. The men, naked except for their rolled sarongs, each with a bamboo basket tied round his waist, stand like sentinels spaced out along the deserted shore watching for a shoal of mullet coming in to feed in the shallows of the surf. At precisely the right moment they cast their net and if they are lucky half a dozen silvery fish the size of small herrings are caught.

Ah Fatt got several more catfish which he brought to the bank using his parang to cut off their pectoral fins, for they each contained a sharp, poisonous spine which could inflict a very painful injury on anyone handling them carelessly. By this time we had been joined by a forest guard and after further consultation the men decided the water was too high. This meant that the otters could find all the fish they needed without leaving the cover of the jungle. In the dry season the level dropped, leaving a series of small pools in which the fish congregated and then the otters were much easier to see.

Not to be defeated, they took us on to Sepayang, an area of semi-deserted paddy fields reached by several miles of rough track further to the south. Lying close to the jungle this swampy area had been cleared by the government, parcelled into smallholdings and given to Malays along with the domestic buffaloes to work them. Some of the farmers were making a go of it but others had promptly sold their buffaloes and returned to the Malay's favourite occupation, a little fishing and a lot of sitting in the sun. Meanwhile their holdings fell into dereliction.

By the time we got there the light was going, the nightjars were beginning to call and the mosquitoes were out in force. Mr Koo warned us that this was a particularly bad area not only for mosquitoes but also for snakes, including cobras and deadly kraits which hunted frogs in the flooded paddy fields at night. A wide dyke overgrown with rushes and choked with water-weeds divided the track from the paddy fields and was crossed at intervals by plank bridges, most of them broken or rotten. Following Ah Fatt across one of them in the shadowy light of the rising moon I remembered about the snakes.

Each small field was surrounded by a bund, and the numerous irrigation channels were crossed by planks, some of them difficult to find in the dark. At the end of one, Keat found the single fresh track of the hind-foot of a short-clawed otter clearly imprinted in a small pocket of mud. Shortly after this Ah Fatt stopped. We all listened and heard the twittering of quite a large group of otters coming towards us in the paddy. Standing stock still we heard them splashing about, constantly chattering to each other as they searched for fish and frogs. On they came, right up to the edge of our bund a few yards ahead of us and we caught fleeting glimpses of their movements and saw the moon flashing on the ripples amongst the paddy. We hoped they would leave the water to cross the bund, but they turned and disappeared back into the dark field. We returned to Sepayang many times and found the overgrown plank bridges were favourite spraining places from which we were able to collect samples for analysis. We saw otters once more in the beam of Keat's torch, but as usual it was sheer chance which gave us our best view of a pair of short-clawed otters in broad daylight.

Jeanne and I had spent the morning swimming and lying in the sun on the deserted beach which stretched away, mile upon empty mile on either side until lost in the blur of the heat haze. The sea was rough with lines of rolling breakers and white surf combing the flat sand where the strand was littered with washed-up branches and trunks of trees, glass floats from fishing nets, empty coconut husks and masses of gleaming white cuttlefish. Shore crabs with long-stalked eyes popped in and out of their numerous burrows and only the inevitable oil marred the desolate beauty of the Malayan shore.

On the way back we explored a rough track leading up into the mountains from the main road. Stony at first, it levelled off with a sandy surface and soon passed through scrub with the stream parallel and some feet below. On rounding a bend Jeanne noticed something moving in the water, so we stopped the car, and getting out very quietly, crept along behind the scrub screen. Two short-clawed otters were busily hunting the shallows, exploring every nook and cranny in either bank with their inquisitive sensitive fingers. We were able to watch them through field glasses without their having any idea we were there, for the wind was favourable and the stream babbling over the stones drowned any slight noise we made. Both banks were overgrown with bamboo thickets and clumps of sedge, and the otters spent some time diving amongst weed where the water ran deeper and slower beneath the overhanging bamboos. Frequently they surfaced with tiny fish, probably gouramis, about two inches long, which they ate in the water holding them in their front paws. They obviously had no difficulty catching fish in the tangle of weed, nor the small freshwater crabs, the size of a 10p piece, which they dug out from beneath the stones along with periwinkles, tiny thin freshwater mussels and other minute crustacea we could not identify. After twenty minutes they disappeared amongst the rank vegetation and we were unable to find them again.

On our last morning in Rompin we were summoned to the bank by Mr Koo. After chatting for half an hour I wondered why we were there and what was the cause of the delay. It transpired that Mr Koo had sent one of his men from the bank to find the Malay owner of the otter we had seen soon after our arrival. Ah Fatt, it appeared, was out getting the exhaust system of Mr Koo's car repaired, the whole lot having dropped off down a rough track when taking us to look for otters. An hour passed and I felt we should find some excuse for getting on the road when the old Mercedes drew up outside and the Malay businessman entered Mr Koo's office. A long conversation followed and I tried to guess from the look on Mr Koo's face what it was about, but without gaining an inkling, for his expression never changed. Suddenly he turned to me and said: 'You can have the otter if you care to go and get it.'

Before leaving with the man in the Mercedes, Keat and I searched several shops for a suitable container without success, until at last we found an old fish basket about eighteen inches square with a wooden lid which I bought for a dollar.

Jeanne and Robin remained in Mr Koo's office drinking 7-Up and Coca Cola until we rejoined them with the little otter, whom I had christened Rompin, safely in her basket.

Our next objective was Chendering, a small fishing village five miles south of Kuala Trengganu some two hundred miles further north. On the way we stopped in Kuantan to buy fish for little Rompin but could get only a rather large grouper which I felt she would be unable to manage. That night we put up at a small resthouse and I smuggled Rompin into our bathroom. Most resthouses in Malaysia can best be described as very primitive hotels, where the food if any is often poor, always local and usually limited. However, the bedrooms are adequate, with hard beds consisting of a mattress on a frame of wooden slats and, if there is electricity, fans which provide a welcome breeze so that it is possible to sleep at night without waking constantly to dry one's sweating face and body on a towel. That is, if the din outside and the noise of men hawking and spitting in neighbouring rooms allow any peace. Sometimes we were lucky enough to find mosquito nets over the beds, though they were often torn. Each bedroom has a bathroom with a cold shower and a loo, the tiled floor sloping down to a drain in the middle of the room.

Released from her basket Rompin immediately scurried behind the water pipes and refused to move. With a blunt knife I had some difficulty in filleting a portion of the tail end of the grouper. After putting the strips of fish on the tiled curb which separated the shower portion from the rest of the bathroom and filling a bowl with water I left Rompin on her own.

When we went to bed I looked in to find she had eaten all the fish and splashed most of the water out of the bowl, so I set to work to cut off another chunk of grouper and while I was doing it she rushed out from her hiding place behind the pipes and seized the other end of the fish. I was very relieved that her appetite was so good, especially when the next morning I found all the rest of her fish had gone and saw her curled up asleep on some newspaper. As I entered she crawled back into the basket and I gently closed the lid. With the aid of some old newspapers I soon had the bathroom cleaned up and swilled down, though Jeanne maintained that the smell of otter still pervaded not only our bedroom but the whole building. It was a smell to which we both became accustomed.

After breakfast we walked to the local bazaar where I bought a plastic watch strap to replace the tight wire round Rompin's neck. Back in our room I placed a cushion on the end of a bed, covered it with a newspaper and lifted the otter from her basket by her tether at the same time giving her a towel to bite. Before she knew what was happening she was on her back on the cushion and I seized her head in my left hand while holding her little hind legs tightly with my right. Jeanne quickly cut through the two heavy pieces of wire round the otter's neck and replaced them with the watch strap which fitted with room to spare. Cutting a four-foot length of tether she tied it to the strap to give us some means of control. Rompin screamed lustily the whole time, but it was a case of being cruel to be kind, and she certainly looked far more relaxed without the tight wire round her neck.

As I carried the basket out to the car I met Robin.

'What have you been doing to that wretched otter? I could hear its screams in the dining-room.'

I hoped the manager of the resthouse hadn't heard it because we might return that way one day.

Rompin, though by no means hand-tame, soon got to know us and for her size had a voracious appetite. As soon as I entered the bathroom she ran towards me screaming her head off until I threw her a fish which she seized with subdued growls and immediately began to eat, often lying in her bowl. She made such a din that I had to be very quick with the fish for fear of disturbing the other occupants of whatever resthouse we happened to be in.

While she would eat almost any fish, she much preferred the silvery mullet, six to eight inches long, straight from the sea, and these I bought from the longshore fishermen, whenever possible, a dozen for one dollar. As the days went by she got much more friendly and we often let her have the run of our bedroom in the morning while I cleaned out the bathroom. She became accustomed to the daily journeys and never made a sound when being smuggled in or out of the resthouses. Only the strong smell of otter never improved and we wondered what the cleaners thought every time we vacated our room.

Hitherto the literature had always been somewhat evasive about the respective habitats and habits of the smooth and short-clawed otters. By now we had definitely established that in Malaysia the former were confined to the larger rivers and to the coast, including mangrove swamps, and the latter to swampy areas, paddy fields, small streams and irrigation ditches. Some of these often get very low in the dry season, but the small short-clawed remain in them, staying hidden in the vegetation. The much larger smooth otter needs the security of deep water with a constant supply of sizeable fish and dense cover on the banks in which to lie up during daylight.

If the two species of otter occupy different habitats, much the same can be said for the Malay and Chinese fishermen, for the former are essentially river people and inshore men, while the Chinese crew the deep-water boats sailing to fishing grounds two or three hundred miles out to sea, just as for centuries Chinese junks have plied south to Indonesia in search of fish and trade. This difference is reflected in their boats, for the Chinese build large seaworthy vessels while the Malays, even on the coast, use narrow-gutted boats and do not put to sea in bad weather.

These narrow boats with high prow and stern are used by the Malay fishermen of Chendering, one of the most attractive kampongs we had seen, lying at the edge of a beautiful bay shaded by great trees. The picturesque fishing fleet lay moored about thirty yards from the beach and the men waded ashore with their catch which they sold beneath the shade of a large ketapan tree where the village street finally petered out in the sands of the shore. Fish of all kinds were brought in, including a huge sailfish more than six feet long with its rapier snout.

Behind Chendering we discovered a swamp of muddy paddy fields and groves of *attap* palms uncomfortably close to a large refuse tip which smouldered with a noxious smell. The place reminded me of Sepayang, and indeed on our second night we saw a party of short-clawed otters at dusk.

The Kerteh River runs into the South China Sea through wild and beautiful country, and since the mountains are close to the shore its course, at least the navigable part of it, is brief. The nearest resthouse was at Dungun twelve miles to the north and as soon as we arrived we heard that the annual festival of traditional Trengganu was to be held on the beach that night.

After dinner we joined the people making their way there. Mostly on foot, the excited, chattering crowds with a large proportion of children had obviously come long distances to enjoy the night out. The beach, festooned with coloured electric light bulbs, was lined with food stalls and packed with endless bicycles interspersed with ice-cream vendors. From a raised bandstand in the middle of the scene a local pop-group kept up a continual chant, joined at intervals by anyone in the crowd who felt like climbing up to sing.

At the far end a traditional shadow play was in action, the moving figures silhouetted on a large white screen and the voices of the male actors uncannily like a Punch and Judy show at home, despite the differences in language. Clambering on to a pile of rocks we were just able to see the screen over the heads of the vast crowd who were obviously thoroughly enjoying the show. We were unable to understand the dialogue, but the action was easier to follow and mostly bawdy, to the delight of the crowd who yelled with laughter when the smart young hero was seized and taken to bed by an old witch with a large hooked nose.

We learned that the shadow play was becoming increasingly

rare and that one of the few men left alive who still made the gaily-coloured figures was called Abdul Bin Draman who lived in Cherating, a village on the coast to the south.

On our way to the Kerteh River we dropped Keat off to do some shopping while the three of us carried on to the kampong which we found at the end of a rough track close to the beach. A primitive notice with the words 'Shadow Play' roughly printed pointed to a path through the palms. Seated on the raised platform which served for a balcony in front of his small wooden house, an old man smoked his pipe and contemplated.

'We are looking for Abdul Bin Draman,' I said, 'and would like to see some shadow play figures.' No reply.

'Are you Abdul Bin Draman?' Again no response. His old wife came out of the house and sat beside her husband. Turning to her I again asked 'Is he Abdul Bin Draman?' The old woman nodded assent.

The flies were biting our bare legs when a young boy on a bicycle appeared and said something to the old man, at the same time pointing behind him where I could see a patch of scrub had caught fire beneath the palms. In desperation I asked 'Can you speak any English?' 'A little,' came the unexpected reply, at which the old man rapped out an order and the boy leapt on his bike and rode off in the direction of the fire.

The old couple continued to sit, seemingly unaware of our presence while we stood chatting and sniffing the distinctive aroma of hashish which wafted on the breeze, and swatting the flies which buzzed in our faces, wondering whether to wait or give up and go. Having delivered his message to other villagers, the boy on the bike returned and I asked him if the man really was Abdul Bin Draman, headman of the kampong and maker of shadow play puppets. The boy nodded and said something to the old man who, apparently satisfied that the matter of the fire was being dealt with to his satisfaction, spoke to his wife who fetched an old jute sack from the house. Taking it from her he took out four shadow play figures. All made of goat hide with arms and legs operated by thin sticks, three were brightly painted while the fourth was still natural leather. The designs were strictly traditional and so was the gay colouring. I could see little point in it when the end product was a grey shadow, but the result was most attractive and a wonderful example of native art which had been handed down for countless generations, reaching Malaysia from India hundreds of years ago. With the help of the boy we persuaded Abdul Bin Draman to sell us two of the coloured puppets, Hanuman the Monkey God and the Hindu Goddess Rama.

The village of Kerteh lay half a mile from the main road on the south bank of the estuary, a tight cluster of wooden houses, shops and shacks straggling out over the water on a crop of stout timber piles backed by sand-dunes and the ubiquitous coconut palms. Aw Joon Wah lived in one of the houses, long and rambling, the river below visible through wide cracks in the floorboards and the air fetid with the smell of mud and raw latex which hung drying in pallid slabs like washing on a line and smelling of stale urine, the result of putrefaction before processing. Like many Chinese in Malaysia, Joon Wah owned a small plot of rubber trees and sold the natural product to a merchant. Comparatively well-to-do, he could afford to send his three sons to Singapore to be educated and his wife was away looking after them.

Taking us into his living-room he threw open the windows and pointed to the edge of the mangrove swamp across the river.

'Sometimes I see otters running along the mud over there,' he said, 'and very often when I am fishing up the river.'

Anxious to find out exactly how often was 'very often' I said:

'If you go up the river every day for a week, on how many days will you see otters?'

After some thought he replied 'On two days.'

Looking down into the water immediately below the window I saw that it was at least ten feet deep and clear. Archer fish, colourful in black and yellow vertical bands and golden tails, were swimming round the weed-covered piles of the house, hovering just below the surface waiting for unsuspecting flies to land close to the water. The fish gets its name from its ability to knock down the insects upon which it feeds by shooting a well-aimed jet from its mouth.

Jutting farther out over the water than the other houses, the windows of the room commanded a view of the estuary down to the distant sandbar across its mouth where white-topped breakers beat the shore, and up river beyond the mangrove to the green jungle on the mountain. In one corner stood an ancient Chinese rocking chair, heavy, ornately carved and black with age, in the centre of the room was a simple table surrounded by chairs of bamboo and on the walls of wooden planks were photographs, formal and faded in sepia of his wife and sons when they were small. A lacquered cabinet containing half a dozen books and three polished conch shells completed the furnishings.

Joon Wah seemed quietly confident that we should see otters when he took us up river the next day and his kindly unlined face with the serenity of a Buddhist monk convinced me he was right.

Back in Dungun Jeanne and I walked down to the fish market after dinner to buy mullet for Rompin. It was further than we thought and we decided to hire a tri-shaw to take us back to the resthouse. Climbing aboard, we sat side by side while the Malay driver pedalled us along the high street. I held my ten mullet, threaded on a sliver of bamboo, over the side of the machine and just as we got up speed the bamboo broke leaving a trail of fish scattered in the road. Yelling to the man to stop, I jumped down and ran back. Two of the mullet had already been squashed flat by passing cars, but squatting down amid the traffic I rethreaded the rest, much to the amusement of the crowd including the tri-shaw man who had turned the machine round and stood watching.

Early next day we drove back to Kerteh. Despite heavy rain Joon Wah was ready waiting for us, standing by his boat at the edge of the water. The weather was so wet and unpromising that both Keat and I decided to leave our telephoto lenses in the car and to wrap our cameras with their normal 50 mm lenses in polythene bags to keep out the rain. As we passed beneath the road bridge on our way up river, the storm increased and despite plastic macintoshes we were all drenched. Huddled next to Jeanne in the bows I hid my field glasses, also in a plastic bag, with my camera under the short fore-deck and tried to see through the rain.

Joon Wah was sure that we should stand the best chance of seeing otters when the tide was dead low, drying out the mangrove swamp, for then they often came down into the main river to fish. At low water the mangrove on each bank straggled across the mud, high on a tangle of spidery roots. There were stretches of *attap* palms, their spiky shoots sticking out of the mud in tight clusters like slender brown stalagmites. Mud skippers and fiddler crabs fled at our approach and once I caught sight of a large turtle resting on a partially-submerged log, but it slipped into the water as soon as it saw us.

The rain lifted after half an hour and as we rounded a bend in the river Joon Wah suddenly cut the outboard motor and at the same time I saw a party of smooth otters amongst the mangrove close to the water not thirty yards away. As we drifted in towards them they ran up the bank and disappeared into the mangrove but after a few moments first one, then two and gradually all six otters reappeared about forty yards downstream, standing in turn on their hind legs to stare at us before sliding into the river where they swam to and fro making no attempt to increase the distance between them and us. As they moved downstream keeping close to the bank, the last otter dived and surfaced with a silvery fish about eight inches long flapping in its mouth. Swimming to the mangrove, it rested its chest on a submerged root and holding the fish in its front paws, crunched it noisily. This caused the other otters to swim back to have a look, giving us an excellent view of the whole party.

As soon as the otter had eaten its fish they swam on. Two of them crossed the river submerged, and reappeared under the opposite bank, while one of the others dived and came up with a fish about the same size as the first, which it ate in the same manner, resting on a submerged root. We paddled the boat across the river and soon all six otters reassembled and we followed them, drifting downstream about thirty yards away, until a man appeared paddling a small sampan heavily laden with prawn pots on his way upstream to fish. The otters dived and we lost them, cursing our bad luck, for this was the only other boat we had yet seen on the river.

Starting the outboard we went off to search for the otters and had gone only half a mile when we found them on the right bank still moving downstream. Cutting the engine we quickly closed the gap to twenty yards, drifting silently on the current while Keat and I took pictures, kicking ourselves for leaving the telephoto lenses behind. The otters seemed to accept us and one of them dived and came up with a fish a foot long which I guessed weighed nearly a pound. It took ten minutes to eat it, resting its chest on a mangrove root as before. Meanwhile three of the otters climbed up the muddy bank and lay on a small promontory at the edge of the mangrove where I was able to photograph them grooming each other's fur.

Having no telephoto lenses, the inevitable happened and we paddled the boat closer than they would allow, whereupon they ran to and fro huffing at us and standing up on their hind legs. Once one of them peered round a mangrove tree and we could distinctly hear it growl. Finally all the otters rushed up the bank and crashed away into the vegetation. Having had such a wonderful view of them for over half an hour under ideal conditions, for the sun had come out, we decided to call it a day and although we made three more trips up river, we never saw the otters again. Joon Wah was convinced this was because the rain had made the river muddy, and the otters preferred to fish in the clearer water of the small streams inside the mangrove swamp.

By midday we were back at Joon Wah's house to collect Rompin whom we had left in her box in the cool of his living-room. As it was still early the four of us decided to go for a swim before having a picnic lunch in a coconut grove by the shore, but as we came out of the water the sky grew black and heavy rain began to fall. A picnic was out of the question so we drove on towards Dungun in our wet bathing things hoping the weather would improve.

When the rain finally cleared we had reached a small village close to the sea in rather pleasant open countryside, the houses scattered amongst low scrub. Nearby was the kampong bandstand and twenty yards away the communal well. These bandstands, found in most Malay kampongs, are used for festivals and other public functions. They consist of a wooden platform about fifteen feet square raised two feet above ground, the modern ones having a roof of corrugated asbestos in place of *attap* thatch. All four sides are open to the elements.

It seemed the ideal place for a picnic in such uncertain weather, but no sooner had we stopped the car than the usual crowd of small boys with bicycles arrived to see what was going on. They all looked amazed when four people jumped out of the car in wet bathing things and proceeded to dry themselves standing on the bandstand! Their surprise turned to astonishment when we produced the Primus cooking stove and lit it, for clearly they had seen nothing like it before. When the food appeared from the boot of the car they were giggling delightedly and really enjoying the show.

It was Robin who finally made their day, for by the time our picnic was finished they had been joined by more of their friends whom they brought up to date on the scene in loud whispers. The meal over, Robin and Keat attempted to wash the dishes at the village well but the bucket leaked badly and it wasn't really practical so they set off for a small stream a hundred yards away followed by three of the youngest lads. The sight of Robin, wearing long shorts, a cigarette in a slender holder firmly clamped between his teeth, squatting in the middle of the stream scrubbing up a rice pan was too good to be missed and they came haring back to fetch their friends to watch this unusual performance.

We had been in Malaysia for nearly two months when Robin had to return to work in England and Keat to Singapore, leaving Jeanne with Rompin and me to visit the last place on our itinerary in search of otters.

The island of Pankhor lies in the Malacca Straits eight sea miles from the small town of Lumut on Malaysia's west coast. There had been several reports of otters from the island and from the mainland in the estuary of the Lumut River. Apart from a couple of tourist hotels at the northern end, Pankhor was virtually uninhabited, virgin forest rising from its shores to a height of over twelve hundred feet, while the Lumut estuary covered vast areas of mangrove swamp. When I had first looked at the map I wondered where to begin and had talked about the obvious difficulties with Ken Sims and Bill Macveigh. While we had been on the east coast they had not been idle. Ken remembered a friend, Mike Oliver, who was manager of a huge and very prosperous rubber estate at Sitiawan not far from Lumut; he also remembered that he owned a motor yacht. Bill agreed to join us for the trip and together they contacted Mike Oliver to ask if we could borrow his yacht. There can be few men prepared to stretch their generosity to the point of lending their boat to three total strangers, allowing them to disappear on the high seas for several days, but Mike did just that.

Sailing round the northern tip of the island we followed the western coast until we came to a cove with a sandy beach and a small, rocky, jungle-covered island to the south. Other small islands and outcrops of rock littered the northern half of the bay. We dropped anchor a hundred yards from the beach where a freshwater stream ran into the sea from a lagoon surrounded by dense jungle. Totally remote and wild, it seemed an ideal place for otters, so we decided to keep watch late into the night, using the yacht's very powerful searchlight. Just before midnight the reddish eyes of two animals moving along the beach were reflected in the beam. Grabbing our torches, Bill and I leapt into the dinghy and rowed ashore where we found the sandy beach criss-crossed with fresh tracks of smooth otters.

In the morning we resumed our watch before dawn; at least five Argus pheasants were calling from the jungle all round the bay, and as the sun rose I spotted a single otter basking on a rock about four hundred yards to seaward. Rowing ashore we landed by the mouth of the stream and immediately saw fresh otter tracks leading up the beach. I remarked to Bill that on the Tembeling River the otters would certainly have had a slide down the steep sand-bank and a sprainting place right on the top. We climbed up to have a look and sure enough there was a large area of fresh spraint deposited during the previous night and we collected a good sample, the first we had obtained from smooth otters feeding in the sea. Judging from the numerous pink shell fragments, crabs were an important part of their diet.

Rompin enjoyed her voyage on the yacht. She had the run of the saloon and galley which opened on to a well deck aft where we kept the box and bowl of fresh water. The sides of the well were too high for her to climb and once we had removed the companion ladder she was unable to get up into the wheel-house, so there was no fear of losing her. Living with us all the time she soon became so tame we could pick her up and fondle her. At night she was confined to the well deck otherwise Bill got no sleep as she much preferred his bunk to her box and her idea of bliss was to swim in her bowl and then dry herself by wriggling and squirming between Bill's sheets.

During the day we cruised along the coast fishing and looking for likely places for otters, anchoring close to the beach at night. For Jeanne and me it was an unforgettable experience to sit on deck enjoying a last drink under the tropical sky, rocked gently by the swell while we listened to the waves breaking on the shore and the calls of the Argus echoing in the darkness of the jungle, so close, yet of another world. It was hot even at night and Bill often had a swim before turning in, diving over the stern to shatter the surface of the water in a burst of sparkling phosphorescence. Only fear of sea snakes prevented me from following his example.

Pankhor is famous for its coral reefs and we soon fell victim to the lure of fish-watching with mask, flippers and snorkel. I shall long remember diving from the yacht to see for the first time the profusion of life in and around the coral. The colour and shape of the reef itself was beautiful beyond belief, with reddish coral shaped like enormous trumpets turned up towards the silvered surface, purple plate coral and gigantic rust-brown toadstools growing on the sea bed, great puff-balls of brain coral bright green with heavily indented surface; the sea bed a mass of spiky fingers, reddish with cream tips or dark green with eau-de-nil tips, the whole reef honeycombed with fissures, caverns and grottoes in which lurked countless fish of every hue imaginable. When I dived clouds of them scattered in psychedelic flashes of colour to hide amongst the coral fingers, disappear into deep caverns or swim through coral tunnels.

Swimming close to the bottom I was able to peer up beneath the overhanging ledges hung with waving weed and stare the shiny red wrasse in the face. It was as if they had suddenly blushed scarlet at being discovered.

The deep, clear water of the narrow strait between the rocky islet and the main island near our first anchorage produced the most spectacular reefs. There we watched fish of all kinds, including pike-like barracuda with jaws full of vicious teeth and cold malevolent eyes. They ghosted round in mid-water, never coming near but never far away, always watching us. A small colourful ray with bright golden bands over its eyes and a peacock-blue stripe down each side of its tail flapped across the sea bed on undulating fins. There were shoals of butterfly fish, fawnish yellow with electric-blue vertical stripes, sea angels or Moorish idols, fish with pale green bodies banded in black, ungainly box fish, groupers of various species, red-barred squirrel fish and mottled gobies lying on patches of sand out-side their burrows which they had surrounded with under-water houses of small stones.

Giant clams, heavily encrusted with coral, weed and barnacles, were almost impossible to see as they waited, their open valves ready to snap shut with dreadful finality on any creature swimming too close. Beds of dark-spined sea urchins clustered together in open patches between the coral. Some of their spines were eight inches long, others shorter like pins in a pin cushion and all of them waved around as if searching for food. The urchin's body in the centre of the spines was quite small, fleshy and pink, surrounded by six small dots which shone like bright blue sequins.

In some places we found large areas of dead coral, brown and grey like rusty reinforced concrete, bomb-blasted and left to rot on the sea bed. It had probably been killed by a layer of sand or mud deposited over it during a series of storms. Fresh water also kills coral and there is nearly always a gap carved in any reef which lies across the mouth of a river, a fact well known to mariners. Living coral is always coloured and forms a layer on top of the dead which eventually turns into coral rock, so that the formation is built up layer upon layer.

We saw no sign of the pest starfish, the crown of thorns, which has destroyed coral reefs all over the Pacific and has reached the Indian Ocean and the east coast of Malaysia. Like the rainbow-coloured parrot fish, it feeds on the coral, eating the living part, the polyp, and spitting out the calcium. Despite several theories there seems to be no generally accepted reason to account for the sudden and worldwide increase in this pest.

On our last morning Bill and I rowed ashore at first light. There were no fresh signs of otters but the smooth sand left by the last high tide was patterned with innumerable tiny marks made by hermit crabs, exactly like the caterpillar tracks of miniature tanks fighting an El Alamein during the night.

In the hope of finding the otters' daytime lair, we followed the freshwater stream inland from the far end of the lagoon, walking bare-footed in the cool water. The going was fairly easy, sandy with occasional patches of sticky mud a foot deep. Soon after leaving the lagoon the stream wound through a patch of mangrove before carving its stony course up into the shade of the jungle. We noted tracks of civets and fiddler crabs wherever there were drier patches of mud but no signs of otters.

Clouds of whining mosquitoes fed on our bare backs and Argus pheasants called on all sides, one so close we could almost hear the bird draw breath before each bout of calling. The bed of the stream cut its way into the hill between huge boulders of rounded pink granite, some of them thirty feet high and festooned with creepers where we were able to walk silently in the shallow water by bending double beneath a tunnel of vegetation. Passing between two such rocks we caught a fleeting glimpse of a male Argus pheasant as it ran up the bank and disappeared into the trees.

Our progress was finally halted when the narrow water course fell from a height of ten feet over sheer rock, a tangle of fallen tree trunks, branches and dead leaves blocking the approach beneath. Sitting on a boulder we rested for a few minutes; a pair of pied hornbills flew over on whooshing wings and settled in a tree close by, kra monkeys bounded through the canopy overhead and a tiny spider hunter hovered before a yellow orchid growing beneath an enormous elk-horn fern on the trunk of a mighty tree eighty feet above the ground.

The otters had clearly moved farther round the coast and since we knew their normal range covered at least twelve miles, it was quite possible for the group to circumnavigate the entire island in a single night if they chose. Such a large territory is not necessarily occupied solely by one pair or family of smooth otters all the time, since the social behaviour of the species allows a loose association with other individuals or groups.

Our stay in Malaysia drawing to an end, only the riddle of the hairy-nosed otter remained and that was solved by a chance meeting with Lord Medway, who was at that time leading a British Museum expedition in a remote mountain area beyond Kuala Trengganu. He had lived in Malaysia and had kept a pet hairy-nosed otter which had been captured as a cub by aborigine hunters in a fast-flowing mountain stream at a height of 1800 ft near Janda Baik in the Bentong division of Pahang.

He believed torrent streams were the home of the hairy-nosed where it fed on the abundant small fish, frogs and fresh-water crabs. Since the species is a typical member of the genus

Lutra and closely related to the Eurasian otter, the cool of a
high-altitude habitat would be the most fitting and would
account for the total lack of records from the coastal and low-
lying areas we had been searching. Clearly it is to the torrent
streams above a thousand feet that future observers must turn
to find more about this little-known otter.

Back at Mike Oliver's we handed Rompin over to Bill who
had offered to care for her and the two young smooth otters
until we got back to England and in the meantime would endeavour to find a mate for her. Despite the problems of getting
a daily supply of fresh fish, not to mention cleaning up very
smelly bathrooms, we were sad to say goodbye to the little
otter and I wondered how long it would be before we saw her
again.

As it happened three months went by before all the formalities had been finally completed and the otter quarantine
quarters at Great Witchingham passed by the Ministry of
Agriculture. Under a recent order otters were included in the
list of mammals which had to undergo six months' quarantine
for rabies upon arrival in this country and we were fortunate
to have our own quarters attached to the Park. This meant we
could look after Rompin and the other otters ourselves.
Furthermore, I had designed the quarantine pens with heated
sleeping boxes and outside runs, each with a large galvanized
steel bath for them to swim in so they would be as comfortable
as possible.

Bill had found a tame young male as husband for Rompin,
and three more pairs of short-clawed otters which we needed
to start a breeding group. All went well until the night before
they were due to leave Penang, when the female smooth otter
from Langkawi was bitten and killed by a cobra in Bill's
garden.

The rest duly arrived at Heathrow Airport, each otter
beautifully packed in its own wire and bamboo crate with a
sleeping section partitioned off at the back and a water trough
made from a huge bamboo split down the middle, along the
front. They had to be brought to Norfolk by a registered carrier

in a special vehicle which complied with the Ministry's rather complicated regulations and it was early evening before the van arrived. Excitement mounted as we opened the rear doors and lifted the crates down on to the grass outside the quarantine pens. As we did so Jeanne said,

'I wonder if Rompin will remember us.'

Bending down, she looked into the line of crates, and Rompin immediately ran to the front of hers, squealing with delight. She was as tame as ever, but had grown nearly twice as big under Bill's care and her coat had a healthy sheen.

Each crate was labelled with the name of the otter and its mate so we soon had the pairs reunited, each in their own quarters where, despite their journey and the change of diet, they ate a hearty meal of herring, whiting, minced beef and raw egg.

11. Watching Otters in Britain

Such is the fascination of the otter that enthusiasts are prepared to endure sleepless nights in cold and wet for the chance of a quick glimpse of one. Much of our knowledge of the life and habits of our native otter has been the result of continuous observation by such dedicated watchers. In south Sweden Dr Sam Erlinge has studied otters in the wild for more than ten years and has gathered a wealth of scientific fact about their behaviour in that country. At home Vincent Weir and Jim Rowbottom are among the most successful observers. But when all is said and done it is the sum total of observations from otter watchers everywhere that counts, and there is still so much to learn.

Actual sightings are rare, but the chances are greatly improved once an observer really knows his area and the movements of otters in it. This can only be learned by regular visits and long hours of watching. Vincent Weir, who has made a detailed study of otters in Norfolk, told me it took him three months of nightly watching before he saw an otter, but then, as a result of his local knowledge, he saw them fairly regularly.

Most of my otter watching has been in Norfolk and around the sea-lochs of the Western Highlands, an area which, quite apart from its own intrinsic attraction, offers unrivalled opportunities for those with sufficient time and patience.

The first time I saw otters in Scotland was sheer luck. I had found what on the ordnance survey map appeared to be a secluded and sheltered cove surrounded by rocky, forested hills through which a burn cascaded on to the shore. There was no road, so leaving the car I set off to walk the two miles or so along a very rough and wet track. The autumn air was mild and damp, heavy with the scent of pine needles and heather. Redpolls twittered in the tops of the pines and parties of coal tits flitted across the path as they moved from tree to tree in search of insects.

The steep slope levelled out a few hundred yards from the rocky shore and the trees gave way to coarse grass and boggy patches of sedge. Only a lone sycamore, gaunt and grey, crippled and misshapen by winter storms, stood alone in defiance of the sea. I was standing looking at the tree when I noticed a movement at the seaward end of a small promontory away to my left. Something was moving amongst the glistening bladderwrack which covered the pinkish, barnacle-encrusted rocks.

Through binoculars I could see two small shapes huddled together a foot above the water. Making a detour inland I was able to approach under cover of dead ground on the far side of the point until, lying hidden behind a boulder, I could see two otter cubs playing together. As I watched through glasses the bitch surfaced amongst the floating strands of kelp and swam to the rock, climbing on to it with a largish, grey fish, probably a lumpsucker, in her mouth. Both cubs ran to meet her and all three were soon sharing the catch.

A few minutes later the bitch stopped chewing and slipped into the water followed by one of the cubs. Both of them spent some time diving amongst the floating weed until they were joined by the second cub which had finished off the fish. It was difficult to keep watch as the swell moved the kelp fronds and I lost sight of them as they moved out to sea.

The shallow water at the edge of such sea-lochs is often thick with kelp, its tough stalks up to six feet long and its wide fronds forming a brown belt along the shore at low tide. The otters find an easy living hunting amongst the rocks for butterfish, lumpsucker and an occasional lobster. Food is plentiful in the underwater forest of waving kelp stalks except when winter storms sweep it away and the rocks lie bare until the new growth begins the following spring.

These coastal otters sometimes move up the burns to visit hill lochs, but since food is never so abundant in such waters they rarely stay long and it seems likely that the visitations are made by young animals in search of a territory of their own.

Bitches sometimes move inland to have their cubs, but more often choose a holt amongst rocks well above the tide line. The holts are usually impregnable, running back into the hillside with many entrances and dry caverns for the nursery.

Adult otters have their territories along the coast just like those living in rivers. Each dog dominates up to nine miles of shore while a bitch with cubs occupies a much smaller area within the dog's range, their territories overlapping. When her cubs are large the bitch travels the full length of the home range which may be up to four miles, so that it is possible for a dog to have more than one bitch resident within his territory.

Bitches with young cubs remain near the centre of their range and only move further afield as the cubs grow older. Dogs wander much more, patrolling their domain to keep rival males out. This they do by a display of aggression rather than by fighting, for as with most animals armed with weapons as lethal as an otter's teeth, there is a built-in inhibition which usually renders actual combat unnecessary, the weaker animal retreating from the dominant. Nevertheless, dog otters do sometimes fight savagely and are said to try to bite each other's penis. That this is so is borne out by Marie Stephens who examined a number of dead male otters and found several had broken or damaged organs. Dog otters have an os penis, a bone which used to be coveted by hunters for watch chains or tie pins and it is this bone which gets damaged or broken when they fight.

Although visiting the boundaries of his territory regularly the dog spends more time nearer the centre. Constantly on the move, his pattern of behaviour adjusts to seasonal changes in the food supply, to disturbance and to the proximity of other more dominant males whose territories may overlap with his. A breeding bitch rarely meets another with a family, for unlike the males, their territories are not usually contiguous.

If otters are not easy to watch, their signs at least make them easy to record. This is not only rewarding, but from a scientific point of view extremely useful, especially as we have so little detailed information on the distribution of otters in Britain, and even less firm evidence of population trends.

An otter on the move within its home range follows traditional routes which connect up with feeding places, holts, rolling or drying places on the bank and, above all, sprainting spots. Every otter knows these routes and uses them whether it is the owner of the territory or a visitor passing through it. The highly-scented, musky spraint is an important olfactory signal telling the otter if a stranger has passed that way and if so, how long ago and of which sex. All otters will go out of their way to visit such sprainting places and to deposit their own contributions. It is this well-ordered pattern of behaviour which makes it possible to keep a detailed record of the movements of otters in a given area without ever seeing the animals themselves.

Spraint is usually deposited beside the water and often where otters come ashore. Certain places are especially favoured – the concrete sill beneath a bridge, a rock projecting above the surface of the water, the mouths of ditches or small streams joining a main river. The sprainting spot is often given away by the greenness of the grass resulting from the regular manuring. Spraint is nearly always left in elevated positions, on stones, tree trunks or ledges on steep banks above water level, often hidden by overhanging vegetation. If an otter has to cross a bank to get from one dyke or stream to another the sprainting place will usually be on the top at the highest point.

Otters sometimes scratch up little mounds of sand, earth or grass and deposit spraint on top and I have noticed that tame otters always manage to produce a little highly-scented, rather oily spraint, even though they may have just cleared their bowels, at the start of their evening's activity.

Once the traditional runways and sprainting places are known, it is easy to keep a check on the movements of otters in an area, but when beginning observations on a strange river or stream I always go first to any bridges, sluice gates, weirs or junctions with other ditches or streamlets. If otters are present spraint will always be found.

Tracks are also useful signs and a look-out should be kept for them in soft mud or sand, especially where a sandbar juts out into the water, as otters often land to cross such a place rather than swim round it.

If the depth of water permits, it is easier to work a river by wading. In winter I wear a wet suit and in summer bathing trunks or the bottom half of a wet suit. For the enthusiast there is always the added interest of trying to identify the prey the otter has eaten by analysis of the spraint. Eels and some other fish are not hard to identify by their vertebrae, but birds and small mammals are often very difficult without microscopic examination of the bones and hair or feather structure.

Quite a lot of scientific data has been published on the feeding habits of otters and from it, coupled with my own observations of both wild otters and tame ones roaming free in a natural environment, some generalizations can be made.

Under most conditions the otter lives chiefly on fish such as eels, roach, rudd, bream, perch, pike and even sticklebacks which, despite their small size, have a habit of forming dense shoals enabling the otter to catch large numbers easily. The otter goes for the easiest and most numerous quarry so that its diet changes according to season and the availability of certain food. Eels, for example, are caught all the year round, but many more are taken when they are active in the summer. During the winter the otter has to root them out of the mud where they hibernate.

In some rivers crayfish are taken, sometimes all the year round, but usually in much larger numbers during the summer and early autumn when the young are about in large numbers and the adults are active prior to mating in October.

Several scientists both in Europe and America have shown that even where salmon and trout occur in a river they form a small part of the otter's diet. Erlinge, working on a trout water in Sweden, found that of the fish taken, trout accounted for less than six per cent, the other ninety-four per cent being coarse fish. Size is also significant and otters seem to prefer fish

10 to 15 centimetres long (4 to 6 inches), though they take bigger quarry such as pike, large bream and tench when the fish move into the shallows to spawn. If the otter has any preference for a particular species of fish, it is determined by its availability and the ease with which it can be caught; thus fish which live skulking lives in dense vegetation and those which swim fast like salmon or trout are taken infrequently.

Frogs are sometimes nosed out of the mud during the winter when they hibernate in pools and ditches, but are more frequently eaten when they congregate before spawning in the spring and again in the autumn just before they hibernate. It has been said that when an otter eats a frog it turns it inside out like a glove, leaving the skin on the bank. My otters have never shown any sign of trying to do this though they often catch and eat frogs – leaving nothing behind. I am sure rats are the expert skinners and I have seen large numbers of both frogs and toads which they have eaten in this way.

Sometimes the otter varies its diet by catching birds, particularly moorhens and waterfowl as well as the young of other species nesting by the water. Moorhens are easy to catch and so taken more frequently, though surprisingly Erlinge found quite a few starlings and swallows or martins had been eaten by the otters he was studying, while I have watched an otter pull down a blackbird's nest in a low bush by the river and eat all the nestlings.

On another occasion a friend and I were rowing quietly round a large private broad in Norfolk, a place much frequented by otters, searching for any evidence that they had been eating freshwater mussels. We found plenty of open and broken shells, all of them grouped in favourite feeding places close to the water, usually under cover of the alder trees, but abundant evidence in the form of droppings and tracks showed that this was the work of coypus.

In the shallow water where reeds fringed the shore, large bream were gathering to spawn, their dorsal fins often cleaving the surface and their tails sending up puffs of sediment as they flicked the bottom of the broad. We found the remains of two several hundred yards apart lying at the water's edge where an otter had dined on them.

Farther on, a spit of firm land rimmed with stunted alders jutted out into the water and as we paddled silently round it looking for a gap in the straggling roots where we could push the boat ashore, we noticed a mallard drake lying on its back in the centre of the spit. Finding a landing place on the far side, we climbed out of the boat and I pushed through some bushes to where I thought the duck lay, but failed to find it. Colin was searching some distance to my left and when he turned back towards the boat I rejoined him, thinking he had picked up the bird.

'Did you find it?' I asked.

'No,' he replied, 'I thought you went to collect it.'

'So I did, but I can't find it.'

Together we returned and looked again, but there was no sign of the duck. Only half a dozen small feathers marked the spot where it had lain. I walked to the water's edge, and was looking at the tangle of alder roots straggling into the water when I noticed a spot of fresh blood on one of them. A few paces away in the soft, black mud, I found the single footprint of a large otter. It must have killed the mallard just before we arrived and returned to collect it from under our noses while we were looking for a landing place. I have no doubt it was still watching us and was probably quite close, but we saw no sign of either the otter or the bird.

I have given my otters swan mussels several times, but they have made no attempt to open them. I do not think wild otters eat them at all, though both coypus and rats certainly do, diving down to fetch the molluscs from the bottom and carrying them to the bank in their fore-paws. The shells are hard and tough to open, but the gnawing teeth of the rodents are better adapted to deal with them.

My otters even refuse to tackle the much smaller salt-water mussels unless we crack them open for them, then they eat the contents readily and seem to enjoy them.

A good deal of speculation surrounds the part played by the

dog otter in bringing up the family. While I have never seen a wild dog otter in company with a female and cubs, other observers have. Jim Rowbottom told me how he watched an otter's holt in a cairn of boulders near the seashore in Scotland. He knew a bitch otter with young cubs was in residence and saw a dog enter the cairn carrying a fish in its mouth. As he explained, this was not proof that the male was taking food to the female and young, for the cairn was large with several entrances and the dog may well have eaten the fish himself.

Another friend, Robert Bauld, who lives on a tiny island in a remote Scottish sea-loch, is a keen naturalist and skin diver. He and his young wife were cruising close inshore tending their lobster pots early one October morning when they saw a bitch otter accompanied by a large dog and her three small cubs about four months old. They were able to approach quite close since the cubs were some distance from the water amongst large boulders through which they could move only slowly and the adults were reluctant to leave them.

When Ripple had her third litter, a single cub, she happened to be in a large enclosure in the Park normally occupied by beavers. She was there because we had been filming her underwater with Gutsy, her mate. I had no idea she was pregnant and was surprised when Roy told me she had had a cub in one of the beavers' empty lodges. Gutsy was sleeping alone in another lodge and so we decided to leave him there and to watch what happened.

During the next week or two we often saw him with his head and shoulders at the inner end of the entrance tunnel looking in on the family. Each time Ripple 'huffed' at him and he retreated. Observation was easy since the beaver lodges have plate glass windows through which the animals can be watched from a darkened porch, the lodges themselves being illuminated by low intensity electric light bulbs. We never saw Gutsy attempt to take food to the family, but he was clearly accepted by Ripple right from the start provided he did not push his luck too far. By the time the cub was ten weeks old she even allowed him into the den, although he still spent most of his time sleeping in the empty lodge or in an extra box which we had provided.

When the cub was old enough to follow Ripple into the water at dusk I used to watch them from the shadows and noticed that as long as Gutsy kept his distance she ignored him, but if he attempted to come too close she seized the cub by the scruff of the neck and diving with it in her mouth, swam underwater back to her den.

Otters are silent by nature, so the watcher is unlikely to hear much of them apart from the famous 'whistle' which, as I said earlier in this book, is really a very shrill squeak. This contact call is used between adult pairs travelling together and between large cubs as well as in the family group between the bitch and her cubs. It is also a distress signal made by a bitch searching for a lost cub, as she will do for hours, or by one of a pair if an accident befalls the other. Should an otter spot the observer standing still in the gloaming, it may surface quite close out of interest, and it is then that its 'huff' or exclamation of surprise or curiosity may be heard.

When very young, cubs inside the holt make a bird-like twitter, especially when the female leaves them on their own; like adults they chitter with irritation as they get older. Two otters getting really annoyed with each other begin by chittering and may end on a rising scale of harsh snarls. If a tame otter makes this noise it means it is very upset about something and is going to bite – as I know from painful experience, for as the naturalist, Topsell, said as long ago as 1658, 'otters are most accomplished biters'.

Another sound I have heard occasionally is the low 'wickering' of greeting between grown animals, a quiet, confidential noise not unlike a badger's greeting note.

While sensibly conducted day-time visits to an area are unlikely to disturb otters, nightly watches may drive them away. If possible they should be done from vantage points where the animals are accustomed to see people, such as bridges or sluices.

Extreme caution should be exercised near a breeding holt,

for the bitch is certain to move her cubs elsewhere if she becomes suspicious. Life inside the holt is secretive, but from my own breeding records and observations I can piece together a record of events including some which I believe have not been published before.

The youngest of my male otters to father cubs was only fourteen months old at the time and the youngest bitch, herself born here, was twenty-six months old when she had her first litter. The only time we were able to record the exact gestation period, the cubs were born sixty-two days after mating, which supports the figure of sixty-one days given by Cocks when he bred otters back in 1881.

There being no set breeding season, the cubs may be born in any month of the year and at birth are blind, toothless and covered with very pale grey velvety fur, their little square noses bright pink. Their eyes open at between thirty and thirty-four days and they develop slowly, being seven or eight weeks old before they crawl outside the holt to deposit their spraint nearby.

Between seven and nine weeks of age the cubs begin to eat solid food, but are at least three months old before weaning, and at about this time they begin to swim. They remain with their mother for a year or so, and from her learn how and where to hunt for food. Even when the family finally splits up, the cubs at first remain close to their mother's territory.

At two months cubs weigh between two and a half and three pounds and at three months about four pounds, males being heavier than females.

This is a brief summary of our knowledge of the breeding habits of the otter. For the patient watcher there is still much more to learn about this elusive, intelligent and fascinating animal.

12. Otters in Trust

Anyone who has had the luck to see an otter in the wild, whether in Britain or abroad, cannot fail to have been intrigued by its grace of movement and beauty of form. Authors like Henry Williamson and Gavin Maxwell were captivated by it and through them the vanishing otter with its quicksilver brain and secretive habits has caught the imagination.

Elsewhere the otter has been caught and killed by the thousand for its valuable fur. Of the nineteen species of otter found in the world, five are already in immediate danger of extinction, four of them in South America where the fur trade booms and threatens to extirpate the world's largest and most spectacular otter, the giant otter of Brazil, which may attain a length of six feet and weigh seventy pounds. Even the more advanced half of the New World is not free from guilt, for the North American otter is ruthlessly trapped for its pelt, tens of thousands of which end up in the Hudson Bay Company's warehouses in London and elsewhere in Europe and America. And just in case anyone thinks we at home are blameless, hundreds of otters are drowned in Scotland every year, their legs smashed in steel traps. And all this to satisfy the desire of Western woman to deck herself in animal skins.

In several European countries the number of otters has declined alarmingly in the past decade and now it is almost extinct in the Netherlands and Belgium and threatened in France and Germany. Even in Scandinavia, where it used to be common in the network of lakes and rivers, its numbers have dwindled.

In Britain and Western Europe pollution is probably the chief culprit, coupled with man's ever-increasing disturbance of the waterways – boating, angling, the canalization of rivers and the draining of marshes. It is the now familiar story of habitat destruction. Like all predators the otter is at the end of the food chain and if fish and frogs become contaminated by poisonous chemicals used in agriculture and industry, it eventually accumulates a lethal dose.

Perhaps the most immediate and serious consequence of pollution is the destruction of all forms of aquatic life starting with the plants and insects, so that the whole character of the underwater scene changes. When the fish population drops the otter may be unable to find sufficient food to survive.

Very often pollution is insidious. Building up slowly it first destroys the most vulnerable plants, so that by the time its effects are apparent the process of destruction is already well advanced. The famous broads of Norfolk are a good example. Where ten years ago there was a luxuriant growth of aquatic vegetation, today the same broads are often bare or choked with blanket weed. The level of nitrogen and phosphates in the water has risen, that of life-giving oxygen fallen, a rich and complex aquatic environment is disappearing to be replaced by a barren waste.

The effects are obvious, the causes not known for certain, though effluent from sewage plants lacking a system of tertiary treatment, industrial waste and leaching of chemical fertilizers from nearby farmland are thought to be responsible. As yet nobody knows where to place the blame.

While the otters of Malaysia are safe for the present, the same cannot be said for those in some other Asiatic countries where the small short-clawed otter is trapped for its skin on a commercial scale.

Otters throughout the world are clearly in need of protection, in need of serious scientific study and in need of support from an informed body of people if many of them are to survive. It was with this in mind that I set up the Otter Trust three years ago with the help of a handful of dedicated naturalists and conservationists who were also fascinated by otters.

The Trust is a registered public charity and its aims as set out in the Trust Deed are:

   To promote the conservation of otters whenever and

wherever necessary for their survival.

To maintain a comprehensive collection of otters in semi-natural but controlled conditions both for research and for the interest and education of the general public and children in particular.

To carry out research into the breeding of otters in captivity with the ultimate aim of releasing young animals in suitable reserves in the wild where such action is considered necessary to reinforce a depleted wild population.

To promote and support field studies of otters in order to collect factual scientific data to help in their management and conservation.

Internationally famous conservationists who supported the new Trust by becoming officers included Professor Grzimek from Germany and Sir Peter Scott, Ian Grimwood and Vincent Weir from Britain.

Soon after the Trust was formed I was lucky in being able to buy sixty acres of land in another part of the country for its headquarters and a home for the otters. The property included a secluded valley with a stream, a small lake and marshes surrounded by open parkland with mature trees on higher ground. It was my ambition to keep some of the smaller Asiatic mammals including deer and wild sheep on the upland.

The site seemed ideal and I came away from the first of many visits to the County Planning Department full of hope. The Planning Officer had listened carefully to my scheme and expressed the view that there should be no difficulty, though of course, the usual application for change of land use would have to be made. With this encouragement I, perhaps rather foolishly, completed the purchase.

In time the application went before the County Planning Committee and was turned down because the access was in the village street. This I was assured was the only reason for the refusal. If an alternative access could be found my application would go through.

Thanks to the kindness and generosity of the farmer from whom I had purchased the site and who still owned and farmed land on three sides of it, I was able to acquire a new access from a minor road outside the village. The Highway Authority had no objection, subject to certain conditions which I could fulfil.

It was about then that I heard for the first time the ominous phrase 'local objectors'; it appeared that the scheme had attracted a number of them. This came as a shock to me for I had never dreamt of people objecting to an otter trust and a park with deer and wild sheep. I had made a serious mistake and the objectors had got a head start. A local amenity society had been formed and letters began to appear in the press and at the County Planning Department. I was told that more than twenty residents in the village had signed a petition objecting to my proposals, and that this would weigh heavily when the Planning Committee came to take their decision.

I immediately organized my own house-to-house petition throughout the village and a neighbouring hamlet. The result was that over eighty per cent of all adult residents in both villages were in favour of the park and had signed the petition in support, a total of one hundred and seventy-two signatures.

Back at the County Planning Department the same official explained to me that not much importance was attached to petitions, only individual letters really counted.

Well, if letters counted letters they should have then, and they did, for out of a total of one hundred and twenty-six residents in the main village, ninety-three wrote in support of the Trust. Some of our opponents became vociferous in their complaints. They talked of lions roaming the countryside, millions of motorists pouring in from the East End of London, a sea of litter, the landscape ruined by cages.

The time was drawing near when our second application was to be considered by the Council, but before that a neighbouring area Planning Committee was invited to give their views, although the site was outside their jurisdiction.

However, after a thorough inspection of the site and a

lengthy debate the County Planning Committee approved the second application by twenty votes to ten.

Naturally, we were all jubilant as we discussed the future and began to make preparations for building large, open, natural enclosures for the otters. Over one and a half miles of perimeter fencing and two thousand posts were ordered, for delivery was likely to be months rather than weeks and already eighteen months had gone by since we had taken possession.

But in any planning application involving change of land use the Minister for the Environment has the right to decide the outcome himself after calling in the application for a public enquiry. In fact, this rarely happens except when large and nationally important issues are at stake. I felt the Otter Trust hardly fell within that category.

But within days one of our opponents was boasting of having put pressure on the Minister to order a public enquiry. Personally I doubted if the Minister had ever heard of the Otter Trust. Be that as it may, the Public Enquiry was duly ordered and for more than a year we waited impatiently for the date of the hearing.

By this time our strength grew as conservation organizations including Friends of the Earth came to our aid. Five peers of the realm from both sides of the House supported our cause. Members of the Trust responded magnificently to our appeal for funds to fight the case, one anonymous donor sending a cheque for a thousand pounds towards the heavy legal and planning expenses.

Visitors both for and against us came to look at the site, and having seen it, few could find any concrete reason for their objection. But simultaneously certain landowners joined forces with our opponents – these did not include those whose land immediately adjoined the Trust, who remained completely loyal to us.

Less than two months before the date set for the Enquiry I met the County Planning Officials with our lawyer and planning consultant. Since the County Council had passed our application, their officers would be on our side at the hearing, an important factor in our favour. At the meeting we discussed the case and our tactics, to avoid too much overlapping which would only add enormously to the cost which we would have to bear. Estimates for this varied between seven hundred and a thousand pounds a day and the case might, I was told, last up to four days. That we could go ahead at all was due to the anonymous donor and to the generosity of our Counsel, a leading member of the Planning Bar, who had offered to accept a greatly reduced fee.

Towards the end of the meeting the senior Planning Officer said,

'Oh, by the way, your application will go before the newly-appointed County Planning Committee next week. I don't expect any problems. They'll probably endorse the view of the previous committee, but if anything goes wrong I'll telephone you.'

Local Government had been reorganized since our application had been granted and now a different set of men was in control.

Four days later we heard that the new committee, without having visited the site, had unanimously reversed the decision of their predecessors and thrown out our application. No reason was given.

We had already spent a small fortune on the case. If we withdrew now I knew we should save a great deal more money. And what were our chances of winning under the new regime? A wise friend with long experience in the centre of the political arena said he thought on the evidence that the Inspector at the Enquiry would probably recommend that our application be passed, but he felt that no Minister of either political party would be likely to reverse the unanimous decision of one of the newly-elected County Authorities.

The following day I withdrew our application.

Friends suggested that we were up against graft and vested interests. I do not agree. There were no pickings to be had. Of the officials I am quite certain every one was honest and fair. Of the rest, some were bigoted, a few fearful for their mortgages, most just gullible.

There was no alternative but to sell our land and to begin searching all over again for a home for the otters, this time not too far from Great Witchingham so that I could keep an eye on both collections, dividing the week between them. It was a tremendous disappointment for us, but the saddest part was having to tell our friends and supporters amongst whom we had cherished hopes of living. Instead we had to bid them all farewell. Perhaps some may have felt that we had let them down, but I honestly believe nobody could have fought harder or more thoroughly than we had.

What will be the future of that secluded and pretty little valley? I hope to sell it to somebody who will love and care for it as we should have done. But it is a faint hope. With development taking place on that side of London, it will probably slowly sink into suburbanization.

As I write the closing pages of this book the film, beautifully produced by Christopher Parsons, has been shown for the first time on BBC television. Called simply 'Otter' it proved enormously popular – even the critics seemed to enjoy it. Six members of the Otter Trust's Council were in it, but the stars who captivated everybody and who won the hearts of thousands of viewers were Fury, Kate and Lucy.

While we resume our search for somewhere to establish the Trust all the otters are living with us at Great Witchingham. Bill Macveigh's nine from Malaysia have almost finished their quarantine period, Fury has recently set up home with a powerful young husband from Skye, Lucy and Kate are turning their thoughts towards marriage, Rhona, Ripple's first daughter, has just had her second litter, three cubs this time, and Mighty Mouse, still in his cardboard box, is squeaking lustily to be fed. Not to be outdone, Mango has just produced four cubs in her first litter.

Otters everywhere need your friendship and support. Why not come and meet some of them and help them all by joining the Otter Trust?

The Otter Trust

Please help us to help otters all over the world by joining the Trust and thus supporting our work.

Members receive regular news-letters, an illustrated Annual Report and free admission to the Trust's collection of otters.

If you are interested in otters the Trust is a must for you and for them.

For full details write to:

> The Assistant Secretary,
> The Otter Trust,
> Earsham,
> Nr Bungay,
> Suffolk

Animal Books in Fontana

JOY ADAMSON
Born Free (illus.)
Forever Free (illus.)
Living Free (illus.)

PHILIP BROWN
Uncle Whiskers

GERALD DURRELL
Beasts in My Belfry
Birds, Beasts and Relatives
Catch Me a Colobus (illus.)
Fillets of Plaice
Rosy is My Relative
Two in the Bush

JACQUIE DURRELL
Beasts in My Bed (illus.)
Intimate Relations (illus.)

HUGO VAN LAWICK
Solo (illus.)

PHILIP WAYRE
The River People

More Animal Books in Fontana

A Fontana Selection

The Sunday Gardener *(illus.)*, edited by Alan Gemmell
Ideology in Social Science, edited by Robin Blackburn
Hitler: The Führer and the People, J. P. Stern
Memories, Dreams, Reflections, C. G. Jung
The Screwtape Letters, C. S. Lewis
Waiting on God, Simone Weil
Butterflies *(illus.)*, E. B. Ford
Marx, David McLellan
Soft City, Jonathan Raban
Social Welfare in Modern Britain, edited by Butterworth &
Holman
Europe: Hierarchy and Revolt 1320-1450, George Holmes
Black Holes, John Taylor
The First Four Georges *(illus.)*, J. H. Plumb
Letters of Vincent Van Gogh *(illus.)*, edited by Mark Roskill
Food for Free *(illus.)*, Richard Mabey
Language Made Plain, Anthony Burgess

Fontana Books

Fontana is a leading paperback publisher of fiction and non-fiction, with authors ranging from Alistair MacLean, Agatha Christie and Desmond Bagley to Solzhenitsyn and Pasternak, from Gerald Durrell and Joy Adamson to the famous Modern Masters series.

In addition to a wide-ranging collection of internationally popular writers of fiction, Fontana also has an outstanding reputation for history, natural history, military history, psychology, psychiatry, politics, economics, religion and the social sciences.

All Fontana books are available at your bookshop or newsagent; or can be ordered direct. Just fill in the form and list the titles you want.
